Crafty Girls'
ROAD TRIP

Crafty Girls'
ROAD TRIP

New Zealand's best craft places
Plus 10 craft projects

ANN PACKER

RANDOM HOUSE
NEW ZEALAND

A RANDOM HOUSE BOOK published by
Random House New Zealand
18 Poland Road, Glenfield, Auckland, New Zealand

For more information about our titles go to
www.randomhouse.co.nz

A catalogue record for this book is available from the
National Library of New Zealand

Random House New Zealand is part of the Random House Group
New York   London   Sydney   Auckland   Delhi   Johannesburg

First published 2012

© 2012 text Ann Packer, photography Deborah and Mark Smith,
maps Lorraine Smith

The moral rights of the author have been asserted

ISBN 978 1 86979 893 2

Design: Pieta Brenton
Cover photo: Deborah and Mark Smith
Printed in China by Everbest Printing Co Ltd

This title is also available as an ebook

Contents

AT THE CONFERENCE

Sydney University 1988

In the midst
Of all the academic discourse
In language fearfully
Intelligent and intimidating
There's a lady
Knitting
Sitting there listening
While her hands fly
In cobweb-fine cotton thread
She is knitting a cloth
For her dinner table
I take the risk
And disturb her concentration
'Excuse me' I whisper
'How many stitches?'
Without
Taking her eyes off
The presenter of a paper
That has me totally confused
She murmurs
'Two thousand'

She has made my day!

In a lecture room
Stacked
With literati from all over
The world
And not missing a word
She is knitting
Two thousand stitches
Into a dinner cloth

Bub Bridger
From *Up Here on the Hill*, published by
Mallinson Rendell, 1989

Introduction

CRAFTY GIRLS STILL ITCH TO STITCH

A road trip. Nothing beats the sense of anticipation, piling into the car for a girls' weekend away — whether you're a Gen X who reads chick-lit in bed, a liberated woman who feels a tad uncomfortable with the 'girls' label, or an 80-something gran who's still a girl at heart — and has never had a problem being called one.

Some of us like to start with brand-new, crisp and clean fabric or wool while others prefer to delve into Nana's scrap bag for raw materials for our quilts, embroidery, knitting, crochet and other crafty projects. Whichever approach you take, there's nothing to match the pleasure of doing it yourself. It's the female equivalent of the Kiwi 'number-eight wire' thing — you start with basic stuff and turn out something beautiful . . . or useful . . . or both.

It's eight years since we first published this guidebook to places that stock everything you need to satisfy the itch to stitch — six since the last edition — and we know it works. We've had great feedback from crafty Kiwis young and old, and tourists too, who've followed in our tracks around New Zealand. Although some old favourites have closed in that time — let's face it, the economic climate has not been kind — new shops continue to pop up, often on tourist trails. While some crafts have lost out to others — beads and scrapbooking have largely replaced bear-making — simple sewing projects such as aprons and carry-all bags have become wildly popular. And everyone can make a cushion!

Shabby chic has given way to a more respectful vintage chic; heartening to those of us who love upcycling textiles because of their link to those who've gone before. We've included in our listings purveyors of antiques, curios, collectables and plain old junk, especially those who keep a basket of linens or a rack of vintage clothes — everything from high-class antiques dealers to opportunity shops, which many small towns have tucked at the back of churches or in low-rent streets.

A new generation of sewers and other crafters is coming through, looking for inspiration, fabric and skills — and there are shops old and new delighted to pass on their knowledge along with exciting new products. It's easier than ever to make your own bag, skirt, baby clothes or even curtains.

There's a new breed of wool shops emerging as younger knitters take up needles. Those who've tried to buy wool overseas will agree our merino yarn is among the world's best — check the label to see where that exotic wool really comes from! We have such a cornucopia of locally spun, hand-dyed yarns to choose from we are spoiled for choice.

Again, we've included places where you can choose something handmade by other crafty people to take home as a souvenir, and since shopping needs energy, we've suggested places for wake-up morning coffees or tea breaks plus the occasional place to eat out in the evenings. We love shops that offer partners a couch to read on, and a cuppa to go with it.

And where we've tried them personally, we've

recommended places to stay the night, sometimes with quilts as part of the décor. Those who've been kind enough to host me are acknowledged on page 272.

Technology has changed hugely since I started out on my road trips. Nothing beats a real map but most phones now will have a map app to help get you from wherever you're stranded to the shop you desperately want to reach. We've tried to list opening hours where they differ from the normal working week plus Saturday mornings — but ringing ahead can save a lot of distress: even the best retailers sometimes have to close their doors for family or staffing reasons. Most, however, will stay open if they know you're coming — though remember, some areas have poor cellphone reception. If you're the organised type, there are also websites; they're listed where available.

A warning: not all craftspeople have EFTPOS or credit card facilities, so try to take a cheque book or some cash. If you miss something you wish you'd bought, most places will mail it later if you request it.

Ever since I researched *Stitch: Contemporary New Zealand Textile Artists*, and revised *Crafty Girls' Road Trip* the first time, the wonderful people at Ace Rentals have loaned me a car when I need to travel for research purposes — including some quite long trips. I'm indeed grateful for their continuing sponsorship.

If you disagree with any of our listings, or have other comments to make, we'd love to hear from you at craftygirl@xtra.co.nz

Ann Packer

Chapter One

NORTH OF AUCKLAND

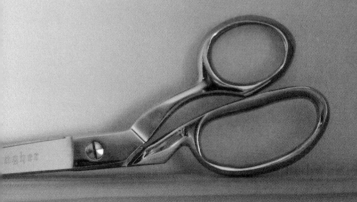

to Cape
Reinga

10

Kerikeri

BAY OF ISLANDS

1

1

Whangarei
Maungatapere   Tamaterau
                    Parua Bay

14

Dargaville   Mangapai

12   Kaiwaka

1   Matakana
Warkworth
16   Puhoi
     Kaukapakapa   Orewa

to Auckland

Visitors with limited time may be in
such a rush they have to drive north
from Auckland without stopping.
But if you can fit in a more leisurely
trip, there are some pleasant spots
along the way — grand beaches, little
bays and historic settlements ... And
places to get your crafty fix, either by
adding to your stash or supporting
the creativity of others by investing
in their wonderful work.

If you're looking for a cheap rental car there are
heaps of places down near the Auckland waterfront. I
use Ace — which topped *Consumer* magazine's survey
a few years ago and happens to be the country's
largest independent rental firm — and I have been
pleased with the service I've received over several
years. In fact, when I approached them about a car for
researching *Stitch: Contemporary New Zealand Textile
Artists,* they offered to become a sponsor. I now plan
my trips around their locations, which are situated
with tourists in mind but are equally useful for Kiwis.

Just south of Warkworth is the impressive *Warkworth and District Museum*, at Parry Kauri Park on Tudor Collins Dr. Maintained mostly by devoted volunteers, it has a substantial collection of pioneer artefacts. There's plenty for kids, including an old jail and an enormous kauri log on a traction engine. The textile collection is one of the best in the country — bathing suits, furs, even a maternity dress from 1830 — and well described on the museum's website. Clothing from Jane Austen's time to the flapper era is carefully conserved by Jenni McGlashen and her team, with a changing feast on general display and the rest stored under calico wraps (viewing by appointment). You can also take a very pleasant walk around the mature kauri grove in under half an hour. (09) 422 2405, www.wwmuseum.orconhosting.net.nz

Almost next door, at 7 Thompson Rd, is a stylish and comfortable studio bed-and-breakfast run by textile enthusiast Berris Spicer and her husband Alan. Included in the very reasonable tariff is everything for breakfast plus home baking, nibbles, juice and all the things you might need on a weekend away. The kitchen area also allows for self-catering if you prefer. Berris, who works as a volunteer at the local information office, knows her territory in detail and can give you all the local guidance you need. Wheelchair accessible. (09) 422 2685, www.ribbonwoodwarkworth.co.nz

Back on the main road is the pretty little town of Warkworth, once a steamer stop on the way to Auckland. Park the car and wander around — there are gift shops galore here as well as several antique shops and plenty of places to eat. As kids we always stopped here for an ice cream, and you can still get big ones at Kowhai Dairy, in the main street. The *Warkworth Craft Gallery* is open seven days. Sadly, the splendid retro and Kiwiana store Mrs Jones has gone for good.

There's a fascinating mix of old, new and recycled at Margaret Hetherington's *Red Barn*. She's been 1 km up the Matakana road from Warkworth for years, but there's a freshness about her refurbished furniture that makes it perfect for the weekenders who flood into the area. Outside, truly old stuff is slowly sinking into the soil — a marvellous trip down memory lane in itself — while further in there is kauri, rimu and oak furniture, stripped back and finished in a manner that suits its personality (including plenty of pale pieces), plus china, crocks, luscious linens and baskets. It's just what a country antiques barn should be like. Closed Tuesdays and Wednesdays over winter. 190 Matakana Rd, (09) 425 8960, 027 473 1318.

Matakana is probably most famous for the *Morris & James* pottery. You can see loads of their classic garden pots at the showroom, even pick up imperfect pots at bargain prices, and they have a pleasant garden café too. 48 Tongue Farm Rd, Matakana, (09) 422 7116, www.morrisandjames.co.nz

Matakana has a popular *Farmers' Market* by the creek on Saturdays that combines produce and preserves with fresh coffee, old china and ice cream, plus a passing parade of ducks down on the shady landing. Charming. Further out, at 1 Omaha Flats Rd, there's the *Matakana Country Park* complex, with more formal market stalls (under cover), a posh café and a very good photographic gallery called *Matakana Pictures*. Lindy and Graham MacDonald's *Red Letter Day* stationery and pen shop — which now has a branch in Auckland's Jervois Rd (see page 36) — started off here, out of their love of 'genuine personal communications'. Matakana Village, 2 Matakana Valley Rd, (09) 422 9748, www.redletterday.co.nz

Back on the main road there are barns galore. Two minutes north of Warkworth on Highway 1 is *Annie's Antiques and Curios*, a big barn full of furniture and quirky collectables and curios. You can also stay at *Annie's B&B*. Open seven days, (09) 425 0995, www.anniesplace.co.nz

An hour and a half north of Auckland, on the main highway at Kaiwaka, is Ngaire Williams' recently enlarged *Apple Basket Patchwork Shop*. Ngaire started off by designing a sewing bag and teaching a class — and it all snowballed from there. She develops her own patterns and runs sewing and patchwork classes and clubs — including one for Pfaff owners — and has a café to boot. (09) 431 2443, www.applebasketquilts.co.nz

Don't be in a rush to go through Whangarei — there's a thriving craft scene here. Local quilters regularly feature in national awards and there is a good patchwork shop.

A billboard on the main highway south of Whangarei alerts visitors to the existence of *Tuatara* at 29 Bank St, a stylish breath of fresh air for anyone looking for good souvenirs and a whole new take on Kiwiana. While the emphasis is on Maori and Pacific work, Tuatara's enthusiastic and talented owner, Kara Dodson, also supports other local artists. The reupholstered retro furniture designs are her own, printed with tapa patterns similar to the sandblasted windows she made for Auckland's Great Ponsonby Arthotel. Screenprinted bedlinen, flax weaving, tivaevae cushions and jewellery crafted of silver, shell, jade and paua are just part of what's on offer. (09) 430 0121, www.tuataradesignstore.co.nz

It's a pleasure to park the car and go for a stroll around the Town Basin along Dent St, the revamped waterfront in Whangarei, which is a good place to pick up some quality craft and relax with coffee looking out at the boats. *The Bach — Basin Arts and Craft House* — is a collective of committed craftspeople offering superb textiles, handmade shoes, ceramics and wood. I fell in love with fine wool and silk scarves by Far North weaver Agnes Hauptli and simply had to have one of screenprinter Ingrid Anderson's pohutukawa tea towels to send off overseas. Open seven days 9.30am to 4.30pm, (09) 438 2787, www.thebach.org.nz

Then I collapsed into the comfortable couches at *Mokaba* café, under the same roof but not under the same management. A great alliance.

Cushla Gavin's *Itch to Stitch Bernina* at 22 John St now has the biggest range of quilting fabric in Northland, plus knitting wools and supplies, and haberdashery needs. She likes nothing better than a weekend stitching with friends — check her website for the mermaid created during a girls' weekend at the bach. They also offer classes and Block of the Month projects, and are always keen to meet like-minded creative people. Open 9am to 5pm weekdays, and Saturdays from 9am to 1pm, (09) 438 7654, www.itchtostitch.co.nz

As you head north, at Kawakawa, inland from the Bay of Islands, the words 'toilet stop' take on a new meaning. The public toilets there were designed by Austrian artist Friedensreich Hundertwasser, who lived in the area for a number of years before his death in 2000. Take

your camera in! Good coffee, too, over the road at the *Trainspotter Café*, named for the railway line that still runs down the main street.

Kerikeri is the home of fibre artist, quiltmaker and fabric designer Mieke Apps, who welcomes visitors to her studio at 851B Wiroa Rd, RD1, Okaikau — but please ring first, in case she's in the middle of dyeing some of her *Spectrum* range of fabrics. If she's not, she'll be happy to show you through her studio, which includes some of the award-winning quilts that have scooped prizes overseas and graced the cover of *New Zealand Quilter* more than once. (09) 401 9797, www.spectrumfabric.co.nz

Jane Webster is restoring *The Sewing Shop*, 66c Kerikeri Rd (formerly Kerikeri Sewing Centre), to its former life as a general store, with dress fabrics and craft supplies for everything from hand embroidery to knitting and patchwork. She sells Janome and Pfaff machines. There's extra, off-street parking on Hobson St, around the corner. Open normal shopping hours, (09) 407 7763.

Right down on the waterfront are the old *Stone Store* and *Kemp House*, New Zealand's oldest standing European building. Built to house the Rev. John Butler in 1821, this simple but elegant wooden house was occupied by James and Charlotte Kemp in the 19th century and their descendants continued to live there until 1974, when the house and most of its contents were presented to the Historic Places Trust. The garden has been cultivated ever since it was first dug in 1820. But for stitchers, the must-see items are inside: the quilts, dolls and other textiles. The Stone Store also sells imported reproduction fabrics including prints, broadcloth, jean, ticking, flannel, satinette, kersey and shirting, and it has authentic milk paint from the US. Open daily from 10am to 5pm in summer, closes at 4pm from May to October. Closed Christmas Day. (09) 407 9236, www.historicplaces.org.nz/en/PlacesToVisit/Northland/Stonestore.aspx

What crafty girl could resist fresh cream truffles, chocolate-drenched macadamias, wickedly sinful toffee ...? At the *Makana Boutique Chocolate Factory* on Kerikeri Rd — there's another in Blenheim — you can watch them make these tantalising confections and taste a few samples before choosing something to take home for the rest of the family — if it lasts that long. It's all handmade, using only the freshest natural ingredients, which means you can't buy in bulk for later unfortunately. (09) 407 6800, www.makana.co.nz

There's a Kerikeri art and craft trail; you're best to pick up a brochure when you're in the area.

Marian and Ralph Logie's dye plant from Akatere Woolcraft, north of Kerikeri, has moved south to dye another day — it's now creating new rainbows at Marnie Kelly's Touch Yarns facility in Alexandra (see page 239).

On the other side of the Bay of Islands, I spent two pleasant nights at Marilyn Nicklin's bed and breakfast and guest lodge *Ounuwhao* in Matauwhi Bay, over the hill from Russell. It looks as if the 1894 homestead has always sat there in its pretty garden, but it was actually moved from Dargaville, partly by barge, in 1992. Marilyn takes patchwork classes in the ballroom in the off-season and made all the curtains, cushions and quilts for the beds. She also preserves fruit from their trees, cooks yummy breakfasts (omelettes, fresh muffins and bread) and will produce an evening meal if you ask in advance. Scattered around the sunny garden there are several self-contained cottages suitable for family groups, that also feature bright and breezy quilts. (09) 403 7310, www.bedandbreakfastbayofislands.co.nz

Across the road are a splendid local museum and the *Bay of Islands Maritime Park* headquarters, with an overview of the regional environment. Along the road is *Pompallier House*, once the Catholic mission. Or you could simply sit with an ice cream on the waterfront and marvel at how peaceful it is now.

Allow a day to explore Russell, New Zealand's first capital — also known at one time as 'the Hellhole of the Pacific' — starting with Christ Church (complete with bullet holes in the walls) and its peaceful cemetery where Maori and Pakeha lie side by side. Walk in and admire the collection of canvaswork pew cushions stitched by local embroiderers, including schoolchildren, that depict local icons.

If you fancy taking the long and winding road back to Whangarei from Russell, you'll be rewarded with some fabulous views, plus the chance to see perhaps the best one of all from *The Gallery*, on Helena Bay Hill. Peter Brown has set up a stylish wooden structure that contains not just a gallery of wonderful local art but also a café that captures the incomparable view, accompanied by superb food from European chefs. Open seven days 10am to 5pm, (09) 433 9616, www.galleryhelenabay.co.nz

It's well worth taking a diversion to Dargaville on the way either north or south. Head west, past old dry-stone walls, from Whangarei for 15 minutes and you reach Maungatapere. Turn right into Mangakahia Rd and drive 2.2 km to *The Country Yard* craft shop and wedding venue, which stocks — appropriately — country-style patchwork fabric and gifts. You can help yourself to tea or coffee and stroll around Kerryn Walker's purpose-built barn, open since the beginning of 2004, and her large country garden, also used for weddings by her photographer husband, Robbie. Morning or afternoon teas are available by prior arrangement. Open Tuesday to Friday 10am to 4pm, Saturday 9am to 1pm. Mangakahia Rd, RD9, Whangarei, (09) 434 6748, www.thecountryyard.co.nz

Half an hour on and you're in Dargaville, where Irene Watson has had the *Wool Centre* on the riverfront Victoria St for nigh on 30 years. She stocks tapestry supplies as well as lots of wool, and she's a knitter herself so you can get advice to go with it. Open from 8.30am to 5pm weekdays and 8.30am to noon Saturdays, (09) 439 7498.

At the *Dargaville Sewing and Garment Centre* on Normanby St, mother and daughter team Marion and Jessica McEwing stock patchwork fabrics, DMC threads and other embroidery essentials. They also sell dress fabrics, including evening materials and laces, with haberdashery to go with it all, and Janome machines. Their classes include lessons for sewers starting out. Open weekdays 8.45am to 5pm (5.30pm on Fridays) and Saturdays 9.30 to 12.30, (09) 439 8540.

There's also an antiques centre in Dargaville, *Suzantiques* at 25 Murdoch St, (09) 439 6775.

And to finish with, how about this for a recycling story — you could call it pulp fiction! A trio of crafty girls in Dargaville set out to make paper out of a pest grass, offloaded in ballast in the late 1800s, which invaded the Wairoa River. *Zizania Paper Mill* makes a tough but attractive handmade paper from the only substantial colony of Manchurian rice grass in New Zealand — and just as well, it seems. The paper is sold at outlets throughout New Zealand. Christine Rope purchased the company in 2007 and moved the operation from the old Northland Dairy Company building on River Rd to 25 Turkey Flat Rd, Te Kopuru, 10 km south of Dargaville. (09) 439 1567, www.zizania.co.nz

My Auckland friend Robyn and I had a girls' day out around the Kaipara Coast Highway, looping out to Helensville and rejoining Highway 1 at Wellsford via

Dairy Flat — wonderful old name, that — before ending up in Devonport. We stopped at quilt stores, antique and collectables shops, and of course coffee places, and finished our haul with a knitting yarn purchase.

We started out at *Quilter's Dream*, Wendy Oswin's business in a light industrial area at Westgate, near the top of the Northwestern Motorway. Like many I've come across, this business has morphed, changing locations and owners over the years — it started life in Freemans Bay as the Auckland branch of Hamilton store Grandmother's Garden, became The Quilt Shop in Northcote under Shayne Giles and now is Wendy's dream come true — and much bigger than it could ever be in suburbia, because the industrial setting means more space for your dollar. The double-height ceiling allows not only for mezzanine classroom space but great walls on which to display quilts. Plenty of parking too. Unit 3, 6 Westgate Drive, (09) 832 6403, www.quiltersdream.co.nz

Then after getting just a little bit lost — these motorways keep extending their fingers out into the countryside — we turned back down the motorway to hit Brigham Creek Rd, the exit to a rural landscape leading out towards Waimauku, where the shiny new Waimauku Village complex sits on the main highway at the turnoff to the old settlement. If we'd had more time we'd have stopped at gourmet honey producer *Bees On Line*, with its café open Wednesdays to Sundays.

Just 700 metres up the road there's a right turn into Factory Rd, then it's left into the shops and we're at *All Things Patchwork* — formerly at Riverhead, now in a big new space in this village. There's plenty of room to show off stock — range after range of bright, fresh and inspirational fabric, including a kaleidoscopic collection of Kaffe Fassett designs covering vintage chairs and couches. It must have been a huge investment in upholstery terms but, as owner Cheryl Houston says, 'I like people to think outside the square!' This shop certainly takes the Wow Factor award for *Crafty Girls #3* — with huge appeal for younger stitchers new to doing it for themselves. A Bernina dealer too. Factory Rd, Waimauku Village, (09) 411 7618, www.allthingspatchwork.co.nz

Within the village is Jo Batt's *The Red Crayon* home and design store, where we found some excellent wee gifts to take home, and saw our first crumpled maps — a great textile idea for travellers, getting round that problem of the crease always being in the wrong place. There's even a New Zealand trio. (09) 411 7910.

We did a brief backtrack to the main-road shopping centre where we spotted an antique shop, full of fascinating vintage smalls — a teazle for the spinner in the family, some intriguing old photographs, wee packs of Air New Zealand playing cards from the days they gave away that sort of thing, and a cross-stitch pincushion, one of many textile treasures in Denise Robinson's *Huapai Collectables* at 322 Main Rd, (09) 412 7299. We bought vegetarian calzones at the artisan bakery next door before hitting the road again.

Heading for Helensville we could almost smell the sea; boats for sale at farm gates suggested it wasn't far away. After looping around where the highway

crosses mangrove swamp, we came into the town itself and had a rummage around *Monkee Business*, in an old butchery at 7 Commercial Rd, the main drag — 'art, collectables & everything in between' is their motto but it's a bit laid-back even for my taste and not cheap. 022 638 4174.

It may have come well recommended, but we found the *Ginger Crunch* café in the old station already closed when we called for a late lunch. So we settled for a latte back in the main street then enjoyed the clothing and felted gifts at fashion designer Donelle Scott's pretty store *Tilly & Lace* — Tilly looks after the store. We were tempted by the goodies using New Zealand wool made in Nepal for Scandinavian label En Gry & Syf, and by the one-off dresses and rag rugs on candlewick. Open Tuesday to Saturday or by appointment other days. 79 Commercial Rd, (09) 420 7811.

We called in to Andrea Miller's *Patchwork Barn* at Kaukapakapa, north of Helensville on Highway 16 — Andrea bought a Birkenhead business specialising in patchwork and embroidery from the cooperative that started it in 1989, and set up shop in a double garage on her rural property. Now Andrea and her husband are moving to Kerikeri, where she will set up shop again — email for details, patchworkbarn@xtra.co.nz

We didn't call on Cheryll Lane, another patchworker whose business has changed shape over the years — she's at home by appointment only at Dairy Flat, on the way back to the northern motorway. After a decade at Orewa, Cheryll moved *Sew Creative* to Albany and now offers a mostly web-based service selling patchwork fabrics and some scrapbooking supplies at 55 Jeffs Rd. (09) 415 7712, www.sewcreative.co.nz

Petite Heart Lavender Bags

Here's a sweet idea. These cute little lavender bags are ideal for putting in a drawer or hanging in a wardrobe.

Simply draw a heart shape lightly onto a 12 cm x 14 cm piece of linen, and arrange an assortment of buttons on top to fit into the heart to decorate.

Before hand-stitching the buttons in place, it's a good idea to lift them one at a time and secure each button with a tiny amount of PVA glue so they don't move.

Cut another piece of linen the same size, and with right sides together stitch around the edges leaving an opening at the bottom about 8 cm wide. Trim the excess off the corners, turn through and fill with lavender. Hand-stitch the opening closed.

Alternatively, the heart can be appliquéd and blanket stitched around the edge with two strands of embroidery thread.

If you want to hang the cushions, attach a ribbon to each top corner with a button. So pretty!

FROM *SIMPLY ROUGE* BY JOANNE STEPHENSON AND JACKIE NICHOLLS

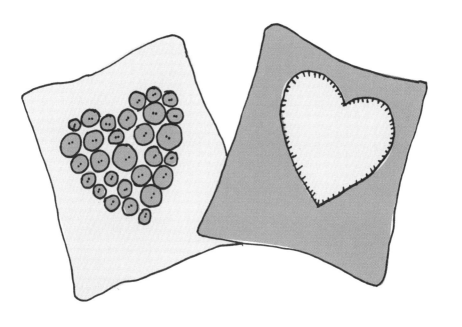

Chapter Two

AUCKLAND

There are lots of crafty places in Auckland, but they're so far apart you can't easily get around without a car. The fabric outlets are no longer in the central city — Smith & Caughey's fabric department and Centrepoint's basement treasure-house in Queen St have long gone — and those that remain are located, mostly, in splendid isolation out in the suburbs, in standalone old cottages, regenerated shopping centres, industrial parks or even brand-new destination complexes.

Many are centred around a sewing machine agency, so you may want to seek out a particular one if you're having problems with your machine. I've tried to tie some of these far-flung places together in a 'day out' format — always remembering that a day out in Auckland means leaving home after the peak traffic (9am) and heading for home before school's out (say 3pm).

Craft Central

The one place on Queen St that I head for on every visit to Auckland is Queen's Arcade, near the bottom of the street; up on the mezzanine is my favourite fossicking spot, *Upstairs Antiques*. Sylvia Anderson's packed emporium reveals more treasures every time you turn around: china, linen, jewellery and collectables from every era, plus vintage (and some new) bears and dolls, drawers full of gloves, buttons and beads, and embroidered fragments. Shop 111–112, Queen's Arcade, Queen St, (09) 379 0887. Sadly, Homeworks, with its embroidery essentials, has gone.

Oh, and if you're after wool in the CBD, *Masco's* is the place locals go to, in the Westfield Downtown, off Lower Albert St.

Once upon a time, Karangahape Rd — known locally as K Rd — had a Barker & Pollock's store that guaranteed a bit of textile therapy in the back room, where they kept their cheaper fabric. Now, you might find silks and lamés in the Indian shops, and maybe a readymade quilt — many of those appliqué quilts you find in posh linen stores are out of India. But the shops that sell Pacific Island fabric have mostly moved, along with the people who patronised them, to South Auckland's Otahuhu, Otara and Mangere. However, *Buana Satu* invites exploring, with its stash of tivaevae bedcovers, crocheted throws, shell curtains and bags woven in Tonga and Fiji. 229 Karangahape Rd, (09) 358 5561.

On New North Rd at Eden Terrace is Auckland's hottest young place, run by a couple of university types. *The Bread and Butter Letter*, named for that charming old-fashioned custom of writing thank-you notes — that reminds me, I have a few to send myself — has caught the imagination of a new generation who fancy stitching it for themselves, or at least buying well-made clothing from the era when people sent such handwritten notes. I took up the website offer of a cup of tea, made for me by the lovely Rose Howcroft, who is finishing a music degree. We talked about where she and co-owner Sarah Firmstone, a landscape architect who lives upstairs, find the frocks and crafty items for sale in the wee shop. They try to keep vintage clothing prices under $30 but find it hard. The shop is currently located in an old block right on the road — but maybe not for much longer, depending on the rental situation. The good news is that the next stop might include a café too. 66 New North Rd, www.breadandbutterletter.blogspot.com

 Global Fabrics has a shop at 139 Newton Rd, Newton, (09) 366 1991.

Across the road at the bottom of no-exit Rendall Place is one of my favourite Auckland stops. Nothing to do with craft but everything to do with classic fashion, *Private Collection*'s outlet at 9–11 Rendall Place has samples, seconds and ends of runs of the latest Visage and Standard Issue labels, including top-of-the-line knitwear and accessories. They've got kids' stuff too. Closed Sundays. (09) 366 1500.

Ponsonby Party

 Down Richmond Rd are several clusters of renovated shops, once dairies and butchers no doubt. *Romantique*, formerly of Birkenhead (there's another in Remuera), is at 98 Richmond Rd, with all things pretty — and some lovely baby

shoes made from embroidered doilies and vintage linen by Raewyn Flavell under the brand Old Soles. (09) 520 2087, www.romantique.co.nz

Further down Richmond at 168 is the legendary *Flotsam & Jetsam* — and some great things do wash up there. I had to buy the Sylko cabinet languishing on the pavement — never mind that I couldn't take it home on the plane. A *House & Garden* stylist came in returning a yellow Tonka toy and a bowls scoreboard while I was there — this place really acquires the most incredibly diverse stuff. Quite fascinating. (09) 361 3831, www.flotsamandjetsam.co.nz. Both these shops had cafés next door, so you're spoiled for choice around here.

Before you head too far out of town, Ponsonby Rd — once the home of pioneer quilt shop *Patches of Ponsonby* — still offers a good half-day's browsing. At 8 Ponsonby Rd is that venerable edifice *Objectspace*, which often features textiles among its applied arts exhibitions — one that comes to mind is Rosemary McLeod's 'No Rules' show a few years ago, which challenged stitchers to break embroidery conventions. (09) 376 6216, www.objectspace.org.nz

About halfway along Ponsonby Rd, on the corner of Franklin Rd, is a small but perfectly formed café called *Agnes Curran*, the favoured hangout of local work-from-home types. It doesn't pay to be in a hurry — they take forever to bring the coffee — but it's a very pleasant spot in which to peruse your morning paper or clear the emails on your laptop, with a courtyard outside under leafy trees. 181 Ponsonby Rd, (09) 360 1551.

Tucked in behind the café is pencil-slim Pebbles Hooper's *Pencil*, which specialises in top-of-the-range stationery. To a Liberty fan such as moi, the

Liberty of London stationery was highly desirable, but I resisted temptation and bought a $3 turquoise ballpoint instead. Beautifully displayed along with the Waterman pens in a vitrine is one of Crystal Chain Gang's immaculately cast glass budgies. (09) 376 8538.

Places like *ShellShock*, at 53 Ponsonby Rd, (09) 360 0324, are the new face of craft, where smart young things — including a male lawyer of my acquaintance can have fun threading up a selection for their nearest and dearest. Crafty girls with preschoolers might like to fly into *The Fairy Shop* at number 79. You must also check out *The Garden Party* at no. 71 with its huge range of pottery, and *Masterworks Gallery* at no. 77 with stunning decorative arts.

Cait MacLennan Whyte was big into knitting way before the renaissance. She's been studying for the past few years but is now back into her home-based business *Alterknitives*, just a short walk from the Ponsonby shops in Herne Bay. She has designer yarns by Rowan and a full range of Debbie Bliss as well as design mags and knitting publications. Cait loves doing mail orders but has no website, preferring to deal with her customers personally. Open Thursdays 10am to 4pm and by appointment. (09) 376 0337, knitit@ihug.co.nz

Red Letter Day, the stationery experts who drew a faithful clientele to their Matakana store, have now opened at Shop 1, 14 Jervois Rd. (09) 378 8085, www.redletterday.co.nz

The Great Ponsonby Arthotel is a perfect place to stay — though not budget-priced. The villa and self-contained garden units are just a short walk away from the buzz of Ponsonby Rd and not far from the Harbour Bridge and points north. Hosts Sally and Gerry are Kiwis, the decor is Pasifika — brightly coloured walls, tivaevae cushions on the beds, bathroom tiles by John Papas and Jeannie van der Putten — and French doors throughout feature sandblasted tapa-design panels by Northland artist (and owner of Tuatara design store) Kara Dodson. In the morning a bright young chef cooks your eggs any way you want and makes fresh tea or coffee to go with your hot toast. You can choose to mix with other guests in the sunny breakfast room or on the verandah, or take your coffee off to the sitting room to download your emails. Off-street parking. 30 Ponsonby Tce, (09) 376 5989, www.greatpons.co.nz

A 15 minute drive from Ponsonby, *The Little Craft Store* in Pt Chevalier is Liverpool gal Helen Trigg's dream come true. She's been crafty since she was four years old, and she came to New Zealand seven years ago. When premises came up for lease near her home in Pt Chevalier, she set up shop selling fabric, yarn and all the notions that go with sewing and knitting. Her hours fit round her school-age children — 10am to 3pm Monday to Friday; 10am to 4pm Saturday; 11am to 3pm Sunday. Helen hosts free knitting groups on Wednesdays and Saturdays, and once a month holds a Stitch 'n' Bitch evening complete with tea, coffee and homemade cake, for a small charge. 201 Pt Chevalier Rd, (09) 849 3295, thelittlecraftstore.co.nz

The North Shore — Birkenhead Bounty

From Ponsonby it's just a short hop to the North Shore, and you could spend a good day out here, fitting in visits to a couple of specialist quilt shops, an embroidery specialist and a needle-clicking wool shop. There are plenty of good cafés to choose from, public art to view and some pretty little shops in which to pick up presents.

I started on Hinemoa St in Birkenhead, for many years the site of the Patchwork Barn, which has since moved out of town (see the North of Auckland chapter). It's still possible to find some real treasures here, all within two blocks and with roadside parking. There are several good places for coffee within a short stroll.

Needlework supply specialists *The Embroiderer*, at 140 Hinemoa St, are into their 26th year and their third building — but say they don't plan to move again. Expert staff can answer most questions, and they've some delectable, and collectable, books as well as kits and patterns for making doll's-house accessories, plus all the usual threads, cloth and kits. Partners Deirdre, Cathy, Kate and Gwyneth produce a glossy regular newsletter and run a Project of the Month, introducing new techniques and products, that's also available to their mail-order customers. (09) 419 0900, www.theembroiderer.co.nz

Primrose Cottage at 100 Hinemoa St smells divine: a blend of rose, lavender and all those lovely natural fragrances. Chock-full of goodies like soaps and candles, baby gifts and jewellery, the shop has been here for around 20 years, although Trish Cornthwaite has owned the business only since 2002. She first supplied Primrose Cottage with handmade Christmas crackers — now she transforms the shop for Christmas from Labour Weekend each year. (09) 480 1634, or email trish@primrosecottage.co.nz

A short drive from Birkenhead, in Milford, is *Crafty Knitwits*, a store set up in mid-2010 by Linda Geor and Kerry Bowles as a local hub of all things crafty — chock-full of knitting yarn, fabric and embroidery threads, plus plenty of kits and other encouragements to start stitching. Their logo is the fantail which, as they point out, 'collects cobwebs to line the nest and make it warm and comfortable, just as we all do with crafting our homes and clothes.' Cnr Milford and Kitchener Rds, Milford. (09) 486 2724, craftyknitwits.co.nz

Delightful Devonport

With its Victorian villas — many offering bed-and-breakfast accommodation — and picture-perfect waterfront, Devonport is a place to stroll, especially on a beautiful day. You can park anywhere in Devonport and easily walk to all your other ports of call — or you could take a 10-minute ferry ride from the city. The ferries go every half-hour.

There are great lunch choices, from the *Esplanade Hotel* on the waterfront at 1 Victoria Rd to *Stone Oven Bakery*, a few blocks up and around the corner on Clarence St — their bread is fantastic to take home too. (09) 445 3185.

The public library in Devonport has a centennial quilt that's stood the test of time. You can still buy postcards of this community collaboration, stitched in 1986. It includes the signatures of veteran textile artists Janet Ryan, Val Cuthbert and the late quiltmaker Malcolm Harrison, a Bayswater resident for many years. There are toilets in the library building too.

A tempting line-up of shops in the village includes galleries, five bookshops selling new or second-hand volumes, including a good range of New Zealand titles, and seven antique shops.

The road down into Devonport has been revitalised with the reopening of the Victoria Theatre and Picture Palace. *Cushla's Village Fabrics*, the legendary Devonport quilt shop, was originally down near the waterfront but has for many years now occupied a building at 38 Victoria Rd, on the left as you drive towards the water. (Cushla herself has moved to Waihi and opened a branch in a splendid old villa — see page 60.) There's a classroom space in a separate mezzanine area upstairs and the shop is arranged so you're not overwhelmed by an in-your-face library of fabric. They cater for dollmakers too. Open seven days. (09) 445 9995, www.cushlasvillagefabrics.co.nz

Right next door to Cushla's is one of the first of the new wave of knitting shops. Fran Stafford's *Wild and Woolly Yarns* at 36 Victoria Rd is dotted with samples of fun projects, as well as the usual stock, and just begs you to pick up your needles again. 'It's like playing in your own toy box every day,' says Fran, who gives away many of her own patterns when you buy her wool. (09) 445 3255.

Down on Clarence St is *The Depot Galleries*, which often has group exhibitions by local textile artists like Auckland Quiltmakers. Open weekdays. 28 Clarence St, (09) 963 2331, www.depotartspace.co.nz

At 14 Clarence St is the incomparable *Ike's Emporium*, where you can buy just about anything crafty for very little outlay. (09) 445 3664, www.emporiums.co.nz

When I'm in a different town, I love the chance to get close to the water. Lunch at the *Takapuna Beach Café & Store* met all expectations — on a beautiful City of Sails day with the Waitemata Harbour sparkling and Rangitoto lazing on the horizon, this laidback sand's-edge café had just enough formality to make a business lunch a very pleasant affair. My lunch companion and I both made the mistake of parking our cars down on the area restricted to cars with boat trailers — oops! — but found space on the street behind the café, and wandered down past the Store where school-holiday crowds were queued up for ice creams. It's designed to be a neighbourhood amenity so is open till 8pm, while the Café closes at 5pm. Open daily except Christmas and Boxing days. (09) 484 0002, www.takapunabeachcafe.co.nz

Parnell, Newmarket and South of the Centre

Back on the other side of town you'll want to have a wander through Parnell and Newmarket, and there are lots of other gems scattered around — they don't all fit neatly into areas, but many are well worth a visit.

If you're down at this end of town at night, *Starry Kitchen*, on the corner of Stanley St and Beach Rd, does a very good Thai meal in surprisingly elegant surroundings for the same price as your average ethnic cheap 'n' cheerful. They do lunch too.
2 Stanley St, Parnell. (09) 940 5678, www.starry.co.nz

In Parnell, *The Fabric Room* at 114 The Strand now has an espresso bar. (They used to have a Birkenhead store, too, but that has long since gone.) I had a good chat with owner Shan Hill — who grew up in the rag trade, going out to visit customers with his dad — about helping younger women gain the confidence to make their own drapes. Most of his yardage is sold for soft furnishings but some will be useful to patchworkers; he keeps a remnant bin by the door. (09) 366 1905. The café looks out onto the green and pleasant surroundings of a garden designer's space.

Parnell is full of gorgeous shops — look for *The French Trading Company* at 2 Heather St, (09) 379 9140, www.frenchtrading.co.nz. Further up at 279 Parnell Rd is *The Yellow Brick Road*, promoted as 'a one stop shop for everything a girl wants', including owner Ruth Garden's Pony Puppy range of accessories and clothing, and handmade stationery by Auckland girls Cocoa Berry. Closed Sundays. (09) 368 4015, www.theyellowbrickroad.co.nz

Pick up some classic Italian bread from *Pandoro* a few doors away, for a picnic on the lawn of the *Anglican Cathedral* across the road — do spend time in the cathedral, following the story of our history through the stunning stained glass windows designed by a quartet of contemporary New Zealand artists. If it's sunny, you'll have an enlightening experience.

Newmarket has its *Centrepoint Fabrics* store —
everything from bridal fabrics to haberdashery
— at 26 Morrow St, (09) 529 2711.

Melrose St has *Martha's Furnishing Fabrics*, a
warehouse full of every imaginable fabric on the
bolt, with its own Supreme coffee outlet on site.

12 Melrose St, (09) 523 3655, www.marthas.co.nz.
Across the road at number 1 is the smaller *Textiles
n Things*, where you might just pick up a bargain in
discarded samples. (09) 524 9784.

The most interesting part of Newmarket is behind
the scenes, in the back streets. It's a good idea to
park the car and wander. *The Poi Room* at 17
Osborne St has a well-established reputation as one
of the best collections of New Zealand designers
working in ceramics, jewellery, textiles and
painting. (09) 520 0399, www.thepoiroom.co.nz.
Across the road is veteran bookseller Doris
Mousdale's inviting *Arcadia Bookshop*, at 26
Osborne St, (09) 522 5211, www.arcadiabookshop.
co.nz. There's also a good little café on the corner.

Gill Ward of *Victorian Gilt* is a legend in vintage
textile circles and her shop at 85 Great South Rd,
near the intersection with Market Rd, Remuera,
has the best collection of antique clothes and
fabric this side of … anywhere. Allow at least an
hour here — and there are some other interesting
stores around about too. Worth a special trip.
(09) 520 5565, www.victoriangilt.co.nz

If I had to choose the prettiest shop I found in my
travels it would be *The Ribbon Rose*, in the wee
shopping village at Ellerslie, on the corner of
Ladies Mile. Heather and Stephen Forlong have
taken over the whole house, full of rooms focusing
on beads, rugs, patchwork fabrics and ribbons to
die for. They host weekly embroidery groups and

have one of the most comprehensive ranges of embroidery requirements in Australasia. While they no longer stock gifts, they own a gift shop across the road in the arcade. 118 Main Highway, Ellerslie, two minutes from the Southern Motorway. (09) 580 2276, www.ribbonrose.co.nz

A few steps round the corner you'll find very good coffee at *Down To Earth Café*, 179 Ladies Mile, and interesting food to go with it. Beware the Ellerslie-Panmure Highway: although a major road, it is a 50 kph zone — and on the national top 10 for daily speed-camera fines.

There's a *Spotlight* store in Panmure, (09) 527 0915 — others in the greater Auckland area are at Wairau Park, Henderson and Manukau. www.spotlight.co.nz

Michelle Cozens is one of the new breed of wool-shop owners — younger, fired up about fibre and keen to share their love with the world. She's been in her shop *Mishi* since February 2010, and moved into 143 Campbell Rd, One Tree Hill, a year later. A knitter for 41 years, Mishi offers evening sessions where people can bring their projects and get help with hassles as well as have time out from the kids. She'd like to do Crafternoon teas as well but that has had to wait. Meanwhile, she says, 'there's a Momo café right next door, making fab food from scratch'. (09) 622 1810, www.mishiyarns.co.nz

Way out at Howick, *Hodgsons Sewing Centre*, which has served the village for over 35 years, has moved into new premises at 16 Moore St, which just happens to be a shop they occupied years ago. They have everything you could need for sewing and craft, from supplies to the machines to make it happen. (09) 534 7301, www.hodgsons.co.nz

Going West

Corban Estate Arts Centre in the old Corban homestead, Mt Lebanon Lane — off Lincoln Rd just before it becomes Great North Rd — is a focus for the arts in West Auckland. There's a shop selling a wide variety of craft, much of it made at the centre, including flax weaving and tivaevae. They also exhibit local artists' work, including some very good textiles. They run a summer school. And they now have a pop-up café, selling award-winning organic fair-trade Kokako coffee, with live music on Saturdays. Yay! Open seven days. (09) 838 4455, www.ceac.org.nz

The Pah Homestead, built between 1897 and 1899 and surrounded by Monte Cecilia Park, is an impressive home for the *TSB Bank Wallace Arts Centre*, which opened in mid-2010. Open every day except Mondays, 10am to 3pm weekdays and 10am to 5pm weekends and public holidays (not Mondays), it offers the chance to see early work by many of New Zealand's best-known artists, bought by meat magnate and arts patron Sir James Wallace. 72 Hillsborough Rd, (09) 639 2010, www.tsbbankwallaceartscentre.org.nz

The Lace Fan haberdashery and needlecraft store may hold the record for the longest surviving business in this book! This Henderson shop has been open nearly 40 years and is still under the same owner. It has one of the biggest ranges of tapestries in the North Island, plus a good selection of embroidery requirements, crochet cotton, hooked rug packs, haberdashery and bridal accessories. Open six days a week, 10am to 3pm, at 16 Railside Ave. (09) 836 3494.

Zoombox Miniatures has everything for 1:12-scale collectors from dollhouse kits and furniture, to dolls and working lights. Anni and Susan's showroom is (by appointment) at 7 Langham Ln, Massey, (09) 832 1698 or text 021 0265 1258, www.zoombox.co.nz

True South

When it's time to head south, Epsom is a good place to start the journey. On a fine day Manukau Rd invites a leisurely stroll past some of the most interesting antique shops in town — the ones that look so tantalising as you pass by in the airport shuttle. If there's no parking outside, try a side street.

 On the other hand, if you find stacks of Sanderson samples irresistible, David and Jackie Frayling's *Classic Curtains and Furniture* has crossed the corner to 409 Manukau Rd — but still on the corner of Queen Mary Ave. David's been stuck on Sanderson fabrics since he started work 50 years ago in London as a 'city matcher', popping into Sanderson's once a week to match fabric for customers. He always keeps a basket of deleted samples for sale. (09) 630 1315, www.classiccurtains.co.nz

 Create is a scrapbooking, card making and paper craft studio and shop at 579 Mt Albert Rd, Three Kings. Access via right-of-way at 10 Warren Ave. Check their website for opening hours, (09) 624 4231, www.create.net.nz

On to Onehunga and the rather misleadingly named Onehunga Mall — it may be semi-pedestrian further down, but not at 355, where you'll find *Patchwork Passion*. Robyn Burgess and Jan Chamberlin tell new customers to look out for the Shell service station on the corner of Trafalgar St, next to the 100-year-old cottage in which they set up shop in August 2003. Seizing the chance to customise their new premises, they persuaded the landlord to leave the exposed brick chimney in the classroom area they've called the Gathering Room, and to take out some walls in the shop area. They have a good range of Japanese fabrics and had the earliest Kaffe Fassett fabric designs in the country; they also have his books. (09) 622 2270, patchworkpassion@xtra.co.nz

Carry on down Onehunga Mall to the shopping centre — you can park on the road, but keep your eyes peeled for pedestrians — and look out for *Antique Fabric and Lace* at 132. There's enough shiny, slippery and sequinned stuff here to outfit the Folies Bergères — it's an Aladdin's cave of gorgeous gussie stuff like lace, ribbons, buttons, bows, braids, fringing, beading and even feather boas to boot. Rising rentals in this truly original part of town may force out such shops — but since these owners also have premises in Otahuhu, you should be able to track them down. (09) 622 2164.

At 151 Onehunga Mall is *Sewing Machine World*, sister of the shop in Hamilton. They supply complimentary tea and coffee plus a whole range of sewing machine brands to use in class free of charge — and they offer over 40 classes. Parking outside. (09) 634 2037.

If you're desperate for a bite — we were by this time, because we got lost in Mt Albert — there's just the place down the road. *Columbus*, at 120 Onehunga Mall on the corner of Princess St, is one of a chain of really good cafés that roasts its own beans. This one's in a spacious old post office with plenty of seating and good magazines as well. The food's inviting too, with interesting offerings like Asian noodle salad, and chicken and mustard pies. I had an excellent chicken and avo sandwich on walnut bread. You can sit outside in summer or gather a huge party together in a separate room. (09) 622 2819, www.columbuscoffee.co.nz

Time to head out to the motorway south and down to Papatoetoe. The name Hunters Corner will ring bells for older patchworkers, since it was there that the late Judy Hewin and her friend Libby Shallard set up one of New Zealand's earliest specialist patchwork shops. On the corner of Great South and East Tamaki Rds in Papatoetoe, just a couple of minutes off the motorway — 15 minutes from central Auckland, down the Southern Motorway; take the East Tamaki exit — is the location for Janome dealers *Stitch & Craft*. It's downsized somewhat but still has everything for woolcrafts (knitting, crochet, rugmaking) as well as jewellery, papercraft and patchwork quilting. There's plenty of parking right outside the door. (09) 278 1351,www.stitchandcraft.co.nz

At Manukau, close to Auckland airport, is Bernina agent *The Crafty Needle*, at Unit 6a, 5 Jack Conway Ave. They have patchwork and quilting supplies, cross-stitch kits and patterns, DMC threads, books and magazines — what more could a crafty girl wish for? They also do sewing machine repairs and run classes. Great parking too, which is not always easy to find. (09) 262 2728.

'May your sorrows be patched and your joys quilted!' is the message from Elna agent *Fabricland* in Papakura, on the street parallel to the main road. They're in enlarged premises at 75-79 O'Shannessey St, where they have heaps of classroom space, used on Saturdays for a wide range of workshops. (09) 298 7295, www.fabricland.co.nz

I love Pukekohe — it feels real. A good old-fashioned working town, 10 minutes from the Bombay turnoff on the Southern Motorway, it has a bustling main street full of owner-operated shops with friendly folk behind the counter — what more could you want? Faye Snook, well known as a teacher in the area for over 30 years, has owned *The Old Sew & Sew* in Pukekohe for the last eight years; she decided to open a business when the town's second sewing shop closed. She's since acquired *Bernina Pukekohe* too — formerly across the road, now next door — and with award-winning quilter Ansa Breytenbach is concentrating all the beading, embroidery and haberdashery lines in the Bernina shop and corralling the patchwork and quilting supplies at 83 King St. (09) 238 6655, (09) 238 7362.

Julie Anderson has moved her business *Michele Ann Wool Shop* along the street to the former Bernina shop at 52 King St, to accommodate more stock for the growing number of knitters out there. (09) 238 7693.

Around the corner at 5 Seddon Lane is Jennifer, Gay and Jim's *Absolutely Crafty*, which has everything you could dream of for scrapbooking and cake decorating too. (09) 238 7695, www.absolutelycrafty.co.nz

There's a good *IHC* store in this block too, where I found a vintage tea cosy; Pukekohe also has a *Sallies*.

From Pukekohe we drove 22 km through rolling green hills to Waiuku, the pleasant small town where Linda Blain has set up her *Jacaranda Fabrics* in a shop painted the lavender colour of jacaranda flowers. Linda, who is known for her forthright manner, may not be an experienced quilter but she is generous in sharing her resources — 'cuppa and cake' sessions encourage quilters, as well as those wishing to make something as simple as an apron, to have a go. She's even taught young local mums to make jam. Linda's dream is to open a retreat — and not just for quilters. (09) 235 0575, www.jacarandafabrics.co.nz

Knitted Laptop Case

Knitted in Pure New Zealand Wool, this is an ideal first project for a new knitter, and guaranteed to impress your friends.

YOU NEED

6 (7) 50 g balls New Zealand 14 ply charcoal wool
Pair 8 mm needles
Sewing up needle (tapestry or darner)
0.5 metre fabric for lining
Sewing thread and needle
2 large buttons & 2 large domes

GET KNITTING

Using 2 strands of wool together, cast on 35 (41) stitches.
Knit every row until the work measures 56 (60) cm.
Cast off.
Sew in all ends.

TO MAKE UP

Wash the fabric lining, fold over and press to size, and slipstitch onto the knitted piece.
Fold the case over, to the size of your laptop, allowing for a flap.
Sew up both side seams.
Attach domes to the inside of the flap and outside of the case.
Sew 2 decorative buttons on the outside of the flap.

laptop size: 33 cm x 23 cm x 3 cm [13 inches x 9.1 inches x 1.2 inches]
(laptop size: 38 cm x 25 cm x 4 cm) [15 inches x 9.8 inches x 1.6 inches]

DESIGNED BY: FRAN DRUMMOND OF WILD AND WOOLLY YARNS, DEVONPORT, AUCKLAND.

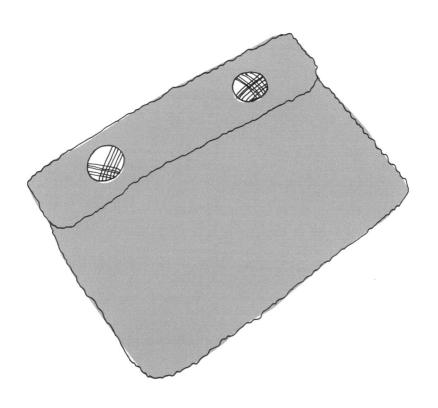

Chapter Three

WAIKATO, BAY OF PLENTY AND TAUPO

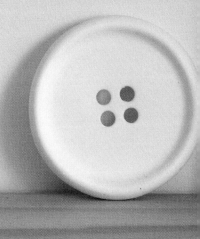

Semco
TRANSFER BOOKLET

EASILY APPLIED TO
MATERIAL WITH HOT IRON

PRICE
1/6

Gently rolling hills, wide open spaces, a mountain or two, the sea in both directions … driving through the Waikato's lush, green pastures is a pleasure. This is the land of racehorses, dairy farms, national farming field days and predator-free sanctuaries. In summer, there's berry fruit at the roadside while out around Te Puke kiwifruit orchards take over. River city Hamilton is at the hub of a network of roads spreading in every direction, with places to replenish your stash, buy good craft and indulge in local baking at small cafés.

Going west, you can treat yourself to a day out at Kihikihi in a country garden. Head for Tauranga and stop along the way at places like Morrinsville and Te Aroha for supplies and coffee. You can carry on down to Rotorua through Te Puke or Pyes Pa in a day if you're pushed — though an overnight stop is worthwhile. Alternatively, head for the Coromandel Peninsula and combine sightseeing with a crafty stop or two.

Hamilton and East

You don't have to travel far in any direction out of Hamilton before you find a shop that offers crafty temptations, and there are plenty of cafés for refuelling the body along the way. It's only 90 minutes to the Bay of Plenty — as long as you don't stop! — and you can make a round trip down through Te Puke to Rotorua in a day if you're pushed, though an overnight stop makes it all the more pleasurable. Alternatively you can head for the Coromandel Peninsula and find some crafty spots at which to replenish your stash along the way.

Starting off in town, you can get very good coffee (the soy latte was perfect) and food from 9am to midnight at *Metropolis*, at 211 Victoria St, in the café and restaurant area known as Southend — the south end of Hamilton's main street. Metropolis have been winners of best café awards for several years running, and their food and drinks — including a good wine list — are excellent. The walls are a gallery for local artists' work. (07) 834 2081, www.metropoliscaffe.co.nz

The southern end of Hamilton's main street is becoming something of a cultural precinct. The *Waikato Museum, Te Whare o Taonga Waikato*, at 1 Grantham St, overlooking the river, is well worth a visit — though Gwen Wanigasekera's five-part *Dream Spaces*, the work that used to greet visitors in the entrance foyer, has succumbed to sun damage. (07) 838 6606, www.waikatomuseum.co.nz. The museum, which has taken on the functions of the region's former art gallery and its museum, has a good café and restaurant and administers the *ArtsPost* shop, nearby in the former Hamilton Post Office — a good place to buy souvenirs and cards. 120 Victoria St, (07) 838 6928.

Down to basics. There are a couple of places right in Hamilton city where crafty girls can get a machine service, extra quilting needles or wool for the latest project. Once upon a time, when quilting was just taking off in New Zealand, the marvellous Pollock & Milne fabric store in the heart of the city offered all you needed. Now it's gone — but there's a *Bernina* shop in the Farmers' Building at 91 Alexandra St, parallel to the main drag, (07) 839 4663, berninahamilton.co.nz, and a *Sewing Machine World* out at Five Cross Roads, between Chartwell and Hamilton East, (07) 855 7467. Sadly, Renee Kim's wee shop has closed.

Knit World has a branch at 651 Victoria St (closed Sundays), (07) 838 3868; and the *Spotlight* store on cnr Te Rapa Rd and Garnett Ave, is open seven days. (07) 839 1793, www.spotlight.co.nz/store/hamilton

Stamping is fun — when I first came across good stamps on a trip to the US, I had to buy some. You can choose your stamps off the shelf at Clinton and Tania Hawkes' *Rubbadubbadoo* workshop, by appointment please, on Mondays to Wednesdays at 248 Grey St, Hamilton East (they share with PBC Accounting). Because they sell at shows, it pays to ring before visiting in case they're out of town. From their profits they sponsor 13 World Vision children. 0508 697 826, www.rubbadubbadoo.com

Remains To Be Scene is a step back in time — like opening an old wardrobe to reveal another era. Ludwina (Nina) Sauerbier has been buying and selling textiles since she was 17, and with partner Ric has had this business for 24 years. Now at 444 Anglesea St, she continues to sell vintage and pre-loved fashion garments, accessories and jewellery, plus other bits and pieces that take her fancy. I couldn't resist the crisply pressed lengths of vintage cottons, including some delicious polished cotton from the 1950s — and a sacking apron too. Open seven days, with reduced hours on Sundays. (07) 839 3086 or email dodgeram@ihug.co.nz

Along the road at 33 Hood St is the well-signposted *David's Emporium*, source of many a bargain for local crafty girls like quiltmaker Gwen Wanigasekera. Everything you could imagine — and a lot you couldn't — can be found in this huge surplus-goods warehouse. Dress-up resources are a special treat. (07) 839 0987, www.davidsemporium.co.nz

Across the road, we had a really good meal, with superb wine service, at Cullens. (07) 838 3618, www.cullens.co.nz

Still in Hamilton, the irrepressible award-winning quilter Donna Ward has *Donna's Quilt Studio* in an airy railway workshop conversion in Frankton — in the street where she once lived in a railway house. There's plenty of room here for classes and her own work, as well as the vibrant fabric for which she's known. Donna's even doing tutorials on YouTube now. 8B Railside Place, (07) 847 3692, www.donnasquiltstudio.co.nz

But let's get on with the road trip. Out westward at Kihikihi — just six minutes from the centre of Te Awamutu — is *Threadbear Cottage*, a charming cottage set in dappled shade in a country garden that's perfect for a crafty day out. You'll spot Isabella — a gorgeous corrugated girl golly made by the crafty Stephen Clothier at Tirau, modelled on ones Julie makes — waving you down. Julie Lealand came by her cottage in a rather tragic way — she broke her neck falling out of a hammock. To help her recovery, her husband and youngest son made her a wee garden house which friends encouraged her to open as a shop. Now fully recovered, she makes dolls, bears and gollies as well as lovely potpourris from her garden — including citrus — and fabric accessories such as cushions and wallhangings. She also stocks her friends' work, from knitting and felting to handmade soaps, and encourages people to bring picnics to make the most of the 1.6-ha area — she'll put the kettle on and provide cups. 91 Arapuni Rd, (07) 870 4450, 027 686 6818 or email stitchedbyjulie@hotmail.com

Nearby at 169 Brotherhood Rd is *Alphra Lavenders*, who welcome visitors during the flowering season, early November to the end of January — and for free. The Parlanes started planting in 1997 and now have over 12,000 plants — as well as 100 roses — so you can imagine the fragrance during flowering. You're welcome to take all the photos you want before the crop is hand-harvested by the family in January. (07) 870 3212, www.lavendergreen.co.nz

At Tamahere Jo Wells' *Hamilton in Miniature* studio is open by appointment to all lovers of things tiny. 285B Newell Rd, (07) 859 2514, 021 241 0059, www.in-miniature.co.nz

We turn our trusty rental back towards Morrinsville on a misty morning midweek, in search of the mighty Milton, who set up *Wright Fabrics* at least 40 years ago. A friend who grew up in the area remembers being taken to Mr Wright's shop with her sister, every spring and autumn, to choose dress material for the clothes her mother sewed for them at home. You can still buy dress fabric there, a good range too — this business was originally bought from Pollock & Milne — plus notions and haberdashery. But I know the cheery Mr Wright as a vendor of quilt fabric at merchant malls around the country, at quilt shows and symposia: I always make a beeline for his stall because he has the best prices. He's big on batiks too. The shop is easy to find in the main shopping block, at 258 Thames St, with a big 'Quilt Fabrics' sign. Closed Sundays. 0800 QUILTS (784 587), www.wrightfabrics.co.nz

If you get to Matamata — where *Crafts 'R' Us* is now that Woollen Wares and Matamata's Quilt & Craft have closed — do stop at *Workmans Café* on Broadway (the main street). We were gobsmacked by their decor, the best collection of fifties stuff ever — transistor radios, postcards, art-deco mirrors — it even decorates the walls of the loo. The food line-up is fantastic and the café consistently makes it onto the 'best café' lists. (07) 888 5498, www.workmans.co.nz

Catherine Cossar's Post Office Quilt and Textile Gallery may have closed but Te Aroha now has *The Framing Quilt and Craft Shop*, started by Karen Larsen and Gayle Bebbington in 2006. They stock everything for quilting, scrapbooking, cardmaking and beading as well as offering an expert framing business — usually the thing that crafters have to go elsewhere to get done — and they teach classes too. No wonder they won the Waikato Top Shop Retail Excellence Awards in the Lifestyle and Well-being Category in 2010. 142 Whitaker St, (07) 884 4590, www.framingquiltandcraft.com

At Waihi there's a branch of longtime Devonport business *Cushla's Village Fabrics* — Cushla opened down here in 2010 in a large restored villa when she retired from town. It's on the corner of Haszard St and Tauranga Rd (SH2), with a large stock and almost as many classes as at Devonport. Closed Sundays. (07) 863 3419, www.cushlasvillagefabrics.co.nz

Plenty in the Bay

By the time we make it to Tauranga, we're starving. We go round and round looking for a park and hoping for something waterfront so we can enjoy the view while we eat, but the town seems to have given that to an endless string of bars, with no sign of anything upstairs that's open. We manage to miss the highly recommended *Alimento*, in the former Masonic Lodge building at 72 First Ave, which sounds just what we like: Supreme coffee, food from the blackboard or ready to go, relaxed indoor and outdoor eating. It just keeps winning accolades. (07) 579 5990, www.alimento.co.nz

By chance, there are several fabric outlets within one city block here. The 70-year-old *Arthur Toye* firm, with its reliable mix of dress and craft fabrics plus haberdashery, moved into 75 Grey St following the demolition of its Cameron Rd premises, (07) 578 2619, www.arthurtoye.co.nz. *The Importer*, another business with half a dozen North Island outlets, began with Asian and Indian furnishings and has since extended its range greatly. They keep a changing range of fabric for cushions and bed drapes — I was tempted by some very reduced sari silks. 79 Grey St, (07) 571 8103, www.theimporter.co.nz

A love of patchwork led Pam Silson to take over *Barnhouse Quilts and Embroidery*, at 45 Grey St, from Marianne Milne two years ago. It's still in the walkway to the Durham St carpark building, and has a café next door — *The Sober Camel* — a combination she says works well for people coming to classes at the shop. Pam has lightened and brightened her Barnhouse stock, with newer ranges giving the shop a fresh look. Quilts by staff members and customers still hang on the walls; embroidery supplies are in a separate, well-lit area and there's a big classroom with Janome machines set up for one-on-one lessons. Pam says younger sewers are buying machines — mostly for dressmaking. Music adds to the relaxed atmosphere — this is my kind of shop! There's angle parking on the street, too. Closed Sundays. (07) 578 7773, www.barnhousequilts.com

Lynette Lauder has owned *Tauranga Knitting Centre* for 17 years and there's not much she doesn't know about wool and what to do with it. She stocks yarns, needles and other necessities for knitting and crocheting at 8/152 11th Ave in 11th Avenue Plaza, as well as online, www.taurangaknitting.co.nz

For a vintage treat, visit *The Elms*, Tauranga's historic former mission house, built in 1847, which has a precious collection of textile treasures. A 10-minute stroll from the i-Site, the house and library in Mission St are open Wednesday, Saturday, Sunday and public holiday afternoons from 2pm to 4pm. The gardens are open daily. (07) 577 9772, www.theelms.org.nz

Tauranga is unbelievably sprawling — no wonder they've built a toll road to bypass the long drive into town. We missed turning left at the roundabout and ended up dragging our way into town, past the *Bernina Sewing Centre* on the corner of 11th Ave at 528 Cameron Rd. The 40-year-old business, begun by Bev and Ken Hayman, is now run by their daughters Glenda and Robyn. (07) 928 5815, www.berninatauranga.co.nz

The other bonus we came upon is the string of op shops (*Sallies*, St *Vinnies*, a *hospice* one) and second-hand shops that line Cameron Rd. On the way back out we caught *Avenue Antiques and Collectables*, 560 Cameron Rd, which has a tempting array of pretty china — including chintzware, which is out of my price range these days. Maybe the tourists buy it? (07) 577 0335. On the outskirts of town, along this strip, are produce outlets, offering the region's finest. Fruit like persimmons and avocados are a reminder of the subtropical nature of the local climate, which is why people retire here. Perhaps that accounts for all the op shops . . .

I first came across Jan Waugh, with her lovely hand-embroidered creamy wool baby blankets, at one of Dunkley's Great New Zealand Craft Shows. She's still going strong, as *Stork Club*, embroidering coloured baby blankets as well, plus sheets, nighties, trendy baby knitting and wraps. She welcomes callers — by appointment only — at her home out at 7 Oakridge Pl, Tauriko, RD1. For those not so interested in craft, Jan says there's about a third of a hectare of garden to relax in — she's happy to round up other locals, put on a morning or afternoon tea and make it a fun day. (07) 543 3118, www.storkclub.co.nz

Lorraine and Barry Langford still live at Tau Tau Lodge, on Pyes Pa Rd out of Tauranga, where they used to run The Country Stitcher shop as well as retreats and even weddings. But now they've let all that go and moved their quilt business into Village@7, a complex at 7 Clarke Rd, Te Puna — a mere 20 minutes away. They've renamed it *Village Fabrics & Needlecraft* to better reflect the type of fabric they carry — contemporary and fresh rather than country — and it's 10 times the area of their former shop. They're pleased to be in a complex that features arts and crafts, garden and living shops, and there's a café too, *Paradiso*. (07) 552 5929, www.villagefabrics.co.nz

Not far out of Tauranga is a family-owned spinning wheel company with an international reputation. When I was in Christchurch I met a spinner and knitter from Bendigo, Australia, who had built a New Zealand tour around a visit to meet the makers of her dream machine. *Majacraft*, at Oropi Rd, RD3, want to make spinning so easy a beginner can do it — but also create wheels like the Suzie Professional that advanced spinners like my Aussie friend will invest in. They also sell braiders for the ancient Japanese art of Kumihimo braiding, and natural and dyed rovings for spinners. (07) 543 3618, www.majacraft.co.nz

Jenny of *Stitchworks* in Omokoroa, as you head north from Tauranga, has branched out from long-arm machine quilting and her specialist wide fabrics for quilt backings and whole cloth quilts to include many other machine-quilting essentials. She also teaches quilting, and will finish your quilt for you. Her assistant Kelly sells designer patchwork ranges online at *Fabric Fixation* (fabricfixation.co.nz). Open Monday to Friday 9am to 5pm; ring first at weekends. 148 Proles Rd, Omokoroa, (07) 548 2260 or 0800 QUILTA. Groups welcome — if you phone first, Jenny will organise a cuppa. Check the map on her website, www.stitchworks.co.nz

Debbie Weal started her Te Puke shop *Sew & Sews* with her dad Nigel Small nine years ago but is now the sole owner. It's the town's one-stop shop for crafters, sewers and knitters as well as offering clothing repairs — 'in fact we mend everything from hunting jackets and bags to curtains,' she says. The shop's easy to find — on the way to Gisborne, left on the roundabout at 54 Jellicoe St, (07) 573 7288. Open 9am to 5pm weekdays, Saturdays 9am to 1pm — or 'if the boss is there, and answers the phone, she'll stay open'.

Carol Biesiek set up her *Katipatch Patchwork & Quilting Boutique* just as the last edition of *Crafty Girls* came out. She has since moved from beside the *Heritage Museum and Carvery Café*, on the main highway just south of Katikati, to an avocado orchard beside a beautiful garden in which you can wander as you wish — why not bring your lunch? There's an extensive range of accessories and fabrics at the shop, which also offers classes for all levels and interests in a large, purpose-built classroom; there's plenty of free parking, and all-day workshops include a meal. Carol is the resident tutor and Cindy the machine expert, so between them they offer inspirational and friendly support, as well as classes with other tutors, both local and national. On Fridays the classroom is open for the day for you to work on your latest project — a great way to be inspired in a social atmosphere. Closed Sundays. 113 Pukakura Rd, Katikati, (07) 549 4775, www.katipatch.co.nz

Over on the eastern side of the Bay of Plenty at 46 Domain Rd, Whakatane, is *Pins to Patches*, where Daphne Green and her team offer expert advice, hundreds of fabrics and a long-arm quilting service. Closed Sundays. (07) 308 9900, visit their Facebook page.

Heading South in the Waikato

Going back across to south Waikato, the view from the top of the Kaimais is breathtaking. When we came up it was too misty; going back we were on the wrong side to stop and take in the fabulous view. Darn. We were headed to Tirau, but getting there was a wee bit of a challenge, because this road less travelled is not clearly signposted and there are lots of sudden changes in direction — but the countryside's all very pretty and we didn't meet any school buses. Windows down on a sparkling early winter day, the smell of silage was overwhelming and stayed with us till we got back to Hamilton.

When we spent summer holidays in Taupo as kids, Tirau was where the bread came from. These days, the town has reinvented itself as something of a craft cluster as well as a comfort stop — a bit like Taihape further south. It's also become a corrugated canvas for local iron sculptor Stephen Clothier. His enormous dog's head signals the town's information office, next to the sheep that houses what's claimed to be New Zealand's largest selection of handcrafted woollen items — everything from sheepskin slippers and rugs to high-fashion merino wool clothing.

Tirau used to be an antique browser's heaven. Now it's more a boutique browser's, with outlets such as Bendon. Lois and Murray Gardiner's *Antiques @ Tirau* is in the middle of town at 28 Mains St, (07) 883 1410.

There's also the family owned *Tirau Shell & Jade Factory*, 40 Main Rd, which is open seven days a week. (07) 883 1230, www.tiraujade.co.nz

Tirau Quilt Cottage, at the top of the hill, is the retail shop of dyer Judi Wine, who produces cottons and silks for patchworkers and embroiderers and designs her own pattern range under the label U-AR-IT desigNZ. She also stocks a great selection of New Zealand-themed fabrics and quilt patterns, books (including extra copies of *Crafty Girls' Road Trip*), magazines and silk paintings, plus local artists' work. Oh, and don't forget the fudge! Judi's open seven days at 17 Main Rd. (07) 883 1133, www.tirauquiltcottage.co.nz

Judi recommends *Beans and Machines* (they roast their own coffee) for the best coffee and a lovely small selection of delicious homemade food.

The big yellow corrugated bear is no longer — nor *The Teddy Bear Maker* shop. It was a big decision, says Heather Germann, to branch out into reproduction French country furniture; the Germanns' new Tirau store is *La Tresor*, at 29 Main Rd, (07) 883 1955, in an 'awesome' position down on the flat. The good news for teddy bear lovers is that Heather continues to make what she calls 'recycled' bears to order. Dressed in fabric special to a family, the Nostalgia bears are made using shirts, jeans, jerseys — anything worn by a loved family member — as a touching memorial. She's just made a couple for children who lost their dad in the Christchurch earthquake. No website yet — just heatherbellebears@xtra.co.nz

Further south, in Rotorua, there are some good choices for crafty girls — first at Ngongotaha Shopping Centre, 10 minutes from town, where *Cottage Flair* is located. Between them, the girls in Jill Brake's team have over 90 years' experience in everything crafty, from dolls' clothes to machine embroidery. They've added wool to their big range which also includes patchwork fabrics, quilting books and accessories, loads of haberdashery items and a full range of DMC, Madeira and other specialist threads. They also have doll-making and beading supplies, embroidery fabrics and kits, Pfaff and Husqvarna machines and country-style gifts. Nice website too — and such a pleasure to share their individual stitching histories. Open seven days. (07) 357 5955, www.cottageflair.co.nz

Across the road is *Essence* café, and round the corner is *The Gantry* café and restaurant, in a 1935 building.

Cottage Flair's Shelley remembers shopping at *Pettits* as a girl — but sadly the sewing and crafts business that began in the 1940s couldn't find a buyer and has had to close its doors.

There's a *Bernina Sewing Centre* in town at 1296 Amohia St, (07) 346 1507, and two hospice shops — at the Fenton St end of Eruera St and 80 Pururu St — among other op shops.

Heading back towards Hamilton, we passed through Cambridge as the after-school traffic got in the way of looking out for antique shops. There are several splendid ones in town — from *Colonial Heritage Antiques* I have a set of silver-fronted milliner's glove drawers bought some years ago that now hold treasured Christmas ornaments; cnr Empire and Duke Sts (the main road south), (07) 827 4211. There are at least three other antique shops in this town, known also for its glorious autumn foliage.

Next time I'll come to Cambridge in the morning, so I can enjoy the pleasant shopping opportunities and stop at the pink, craft-filled *Country Store* at 92 Victoria St. Their upstairs café — formerly All Saints, after the original church, but now *Toccata Café* — is open every day except Christmas Day, from 8.30am (9.30am on Sundays) to 5pm. (07) 827 8715, www.cambridgecountrystore.co.nz

Bev Johnson's *Quilters Patch* has moved round to the main street — Shop 5, 39 Victoria St — so she can have more fabric, a bigger classroom and space for her assistant Jenny to do long-arm quilting on site.

She runs Sit and Sew sessions in which stitchers can work on their own projects, and her Midnight UFO (Unfinished Fabric Objects) gatherings are popular too. Quilts around the walls bring people in just to look — and there's a Robert Harris café next door. (07) 823 5878, www.quilterspatch.co.nz

Duck back to the crossroads and continue north on the Taupiri bypass, SH18 (the scenic route, also known as the long and winding way) to *Grandmother's Garden* at Gordonton. Hazel Wolff opened her business in a suburban shopping centre in 1984, after returning from the US, and moved to Gordonton some 14 years later. New Zealand's largest quilt shop, it stocks around 5000 bolts of fabric and has a huge mail-order business. There's on-site parking around the corner behind the basement shop, under Hazel's house at 1042 Gordonton Rd, where it meets Woodlands Rd. Inside, the shop has fabric in every nook and cranny, with women cutting and packing material for mail orders, making quilts and designing new ones. Grandmother's Garden makes sorties to other centres in the North and South islands every so often — check their website. They are open 9am to 5pm daily except for some statutory holidays. (07) 824 3050, www.grandmothers.co.nz

If you're dying for a cuppa before the 15-minute trip back to Hamilton, next door is *Willow Glen* restaurant and wine bar, overlooking the garden developed by guru Eion Scarrow some 20 years ago. You can enjoy coffee or lunch on the deck and wander in the gardens. Summer opening hours Wednesdays to Sundays 10am to 3pm. 934 Gordonton Rd, (07) 824 3691, www.willowglen.co.nz

Coromandel Capers

Out on the Hauraki Plains at Paeroa is *Patches & Cream*. Pamela Blaikie's business grew out of *Gold'N'Views*, Pamela and her husband Nigel's quilt-laden bed and breakfast establishment. She set up shop in a side street then moved to larger premises on the town's main street. With over 40 years in the rag trade Pam has experience in everything from making dolls' clothes as a child to soft furnishings and a Benson and Hedges Fashion Award entry — but patchwork is her passion. She'll even organise complimentary tea and scones for bus loads by arrangement. Next to the National Bank at 100 Normanby Rd, closed Sundays, 0800 023 259, www.patchesandcream.co.nz

Brenda's Craft Cupboard in Thames is just that, she says — the size of a cupboard — 'But we have a lot in here!' That includes curtaining, ribbon, lace and buttons, as well as patchwork fabric and wool.

She took over from the previous owners in 2005 but has worked in the shop 'forever'. Open 9am to 5pm weekdays and 9am to 12 noon Saturdays.

On the main road, at 468 Pollen St, Thames, (07) 868 8190. Brenda's favourite café is *Food for Thought* along the street.

The road to the town of Coromandel, 55 km north, winds past pretty bays that in early summer are ablaze with pohutukawa blossom, source of much inspiration for quilters, embroiderers and knitters.

In the main street of Coromandel Town, at 151 Kapanga Rd, is longtime local stalwart *Stapleton's of Coromandel*, which has a good range of patchwork fabric as well as haberdashery. They also sell vibrant appliqué cushion kits featuring New Zealand birds using New Zealand-themed batik fabrics. (07) 866 8700.

Down the road at 46 Kapanga Rd, *Weta Design* has great work by local artists, including sculpture and some stunning jewellery; (07) 866 8823. And there's good food and coffee seven days a week from 10am at the *Peppertree Restaurant and Bar*, (07) 866 8211, www.peppertreerestaurant.co.nz

Time out: if you've got children with you, drive 3 km north of town to ceramicist Barry Brickell's *Driving Creek Railway*, where you can take an hour-long trip on the railway the veteran potter built to transport his raw material. From the 'Eyefull Tower' at the top, you can see forever — or at least to Auckland's Sky Tower. (07) 866 8703, www.drivingcreekrailway.co.nz

If you want to venture to the other side of the peninsula, the main road to Whitianga follows the coast for much of the way, and takes about an hour — if you don't stop to smell the sea air.

You'll certainly be ready for something to eat now. My pick is *Café Nina*, in a century-old miner's cottage at 20 Victoria St, behind the Whitianga Library. They have strong coffee and excellent home-cooked food. Best of all, you can eat outdoors in summer, or by the fire in winter. Open seven days for breakfast and lunch. (07) 866 5440.

South from Tirau

If you're heading south from Tirau to Taupo, here are a few craft shops for you to check out, though I haven't been able to travel that route myself this time round.

In Putaruru is Janice Keijzer's *Quilt and Knit 2*, at 21 Arapuni St. She has everything for quilters and knitters, plus haberdashery, and had been in her shop just a year when I phoned her for a chat. (07) 883 7673.

Di's Patch, the patchwork shop in Tokoroa, has closed, but *Knit n Purl* wool shop at 47 Bridge St has wool and haby and is open weekdays 10am to 4.30pm. (07) 886 5608.

Taupo's the kind of place that makes me itch to stitch. Perhaps it's the combination of all that marvellous scenery and being on holiday. Over the years I've knitted jerseys, crocheted peggy squares and pieced quilts at Taupo — always with the lake and the mountains as a backdrop.

The stats show that Taupo's population increases tenfold during holiday periods and most visitors shop at least once during their stay. Crafty girls may up the average. The 2012 biennial national quilt symposium is being held in Taupo, assisted by a passionate group of local textile artists called *Fibres Unlimited*, who exhibit every second year at the *Lake Taupo Museum and Art Gallery* — worth checking out because it often has fibre exhibitions. Story Pl, off Tongariro St, which leads down to the lake, (07) 376 0414. The stitchers, coordinated by Pene Williamson, started as part of the Taupo Society of Arts but have been joined by others from out of the area.

Crafty girls can get supplies at *Clever Hands*, the patchwork shop and Bernina specialist at 32 Spa Rd, just up from Countdown, on the road going up to the famous AC Baths. Dianne Traveller is the stitcher, and her husband Gary is the sewing machine technician — there's a long-arm quilter on site too. They've been open since October 2008 and stock plenty of bright fabrics for contemporary quilts and homewares. Their classroom, which teaches everything from beginner patchwork, fills up with school kids in the holidays. Open seven days. (07) 376 8269, www.cleverhands.co.nz

If you're after knitting wool, check out *The Wool Shed*, cnr Ruapehu and Paorahapi Sts, (07) 378 9513; it sells everything woolly; or *Fabryx*, up at Unit 5A, 29 Totara St, Tauhara. (07) 376 7494.

At 45 Heu Heu St is *Replete*, my favourite coffee place, which consistently wins accolades. Its sunny wide-open windows offer the perfect spot to write some postcards or read the paper. Actually, Taupo is full of good places for coffee, including some on the lakefront with great views. (07) 378 0606.

Kura, at 47A, next to *Replete*, has great New Zealand craft to buy. (07) 377 4068, www.kura.co.nz

Crochet Necklace

YOU WILL NEED

1.5 mm crochet hook – if using cotton, obtain a cotton hook
10 g of 4 ply yarn

INSTRUCTIONS

With the 1.5 mm hook, make a chain. Slip stitch in the 1st chain to make a circle.

Make 2 chain, 2 treble, 2 chain and slip stitch into the circle.

Repeat from * to * 5 times. Join with a slip stitch into the 2nd chain.

This makes a 5-petal flower.

Make 6 or 8 chain stitches between the flowers.
Repeat these two steps until the necklace is the desired length.

DESIGNED BY: NICOLA BOTA OF KNITCOLA STITCHERY, ASHBURTON

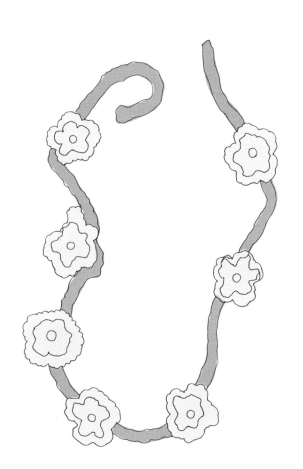

Chapter Four

THE EAST COAST OF
THE NORTH ISLAND

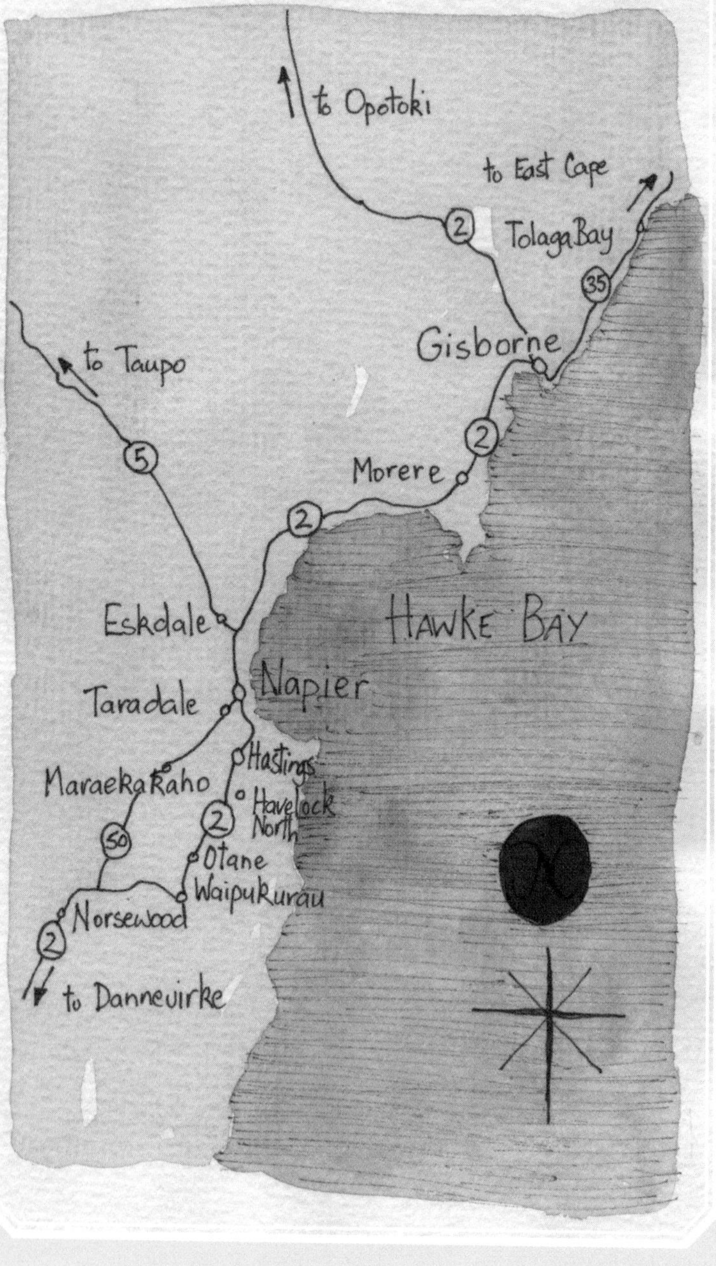
to Opotoki
to East Cape
Tolaga Bay
35
2
Gisborne
to Taupo
5
Morere
2
HAWKE BAY
Eskdale
Napier
Taradale
Hastings
Maraekakaho
Havelock North
50
Otane
Waipukurau
Norsewood
to Dannevirke

Te Tairawhiti — 'the coast where the sun shines across the waters'. It seems a much better name than Poverty Bay, Captain Cook's label for the region that now produces award-winning chardonnays and fabulous food, and has some of the best surf breaks in the country.

The river flats you cross coming into Gisborne from the south have seen some turbulent history. Step inside Matawhero Church, just off Highway 2 on the outskirts of town, and you're back in the past. Still used for Presbyterian services, the church was built as a schoolroom in 1865 and has been variously used for Anglican worship, as a schoolroom, a meeting place and a hospital. It was the only building to survive the Poverty Bay massacre by Te Kooti on 10 November 1868.The lobby houses a community banner stitched to celebrate both the national sesquicentenary, 1990, and 150 years of worship in the community. Small vignettes handstitched by parishioners tell the story of the parish and its surrounding area. Gisborne's a good base from which to make daily forays up the coast — although the craft scene here is not well established. The pace of life may be laidback but the city itself is on the edge of a curler, with heritage buildings, such as the Poverty Bay Club, opening as restaurants and boutique hotels, a wharf shed converted into a fresh produce market, and harbour-front buildings opening up to the sea in a string of watering and eating holes.

This time I was travelling with Den, my husband, and we stayed with ex-Wellington friends at *Endeavour Lodge* motel on the main street, 525 Gladstone Rd. Simple but adequate, it's got a pool that stays cool in the heat of summer and you can leave the windows in your unit open all the time. There are flasher places, but staying here meant we could spend some cash on fabric and food. (06) 868 6075.

The heart of Gisborne — Gizzy to the locals — is surprisingly leafy, with established deciduous trees on streets, parks and gardens. The CBD has lost its wild west flavour to a new design that includes plentiful palms and wide, shady verandahs.

We enjoyed our coffee fix at *Muirs*, 62 Gladstone Rd, a more-than-century-old bookshop owned till recently by the Muir family, which has an upstairs café opening onto a balcony. The room's been stripped back to bare boards and brick walls, there are newspapers and mags to read and you're surrounded by books. The air-conditioning and ceiling fans keep you cool on the hottest summer days while you sip Supreme lattes and read the *Dominion Post* — some Wellington essentials we just can't do without. Check out Muirs' craft books downstairs. Open seven days. (06) 867 9741.

Mercados Gallery houses the collective known as Carpe Diem, which sells work including flax kete and Heirloom Weavers' mohair rugs in the heart of the main street, 57 Gladstone Rd. (06) 868 8814.

Bird of Prey, formerly Bex, has moved into a heritage building at 25B Fitzherbert St where Amanda Laidlaw-May continues to support New Zealand artists and craftspeople, selling Maori weaving, shells, lavender products, designer and recycled clothing, and jewellery, including her own brand Bird of Prey. The Edwardian bay villa, which used to house the Town and Countrywomen's Club, features old-fashioned tea rooms and there are plans for studios upstairs for artists and holistic practitioners. Phone to check opening hours. (06) 867 8511, www.birdofprey.co.nz

Retro is Ro Darrall's shop selling mid-century goodies — stuff from the fifties and sixties including fabrics, buttons and clothes, 'a bit of everything really', at 8 Ballance St, in the Ballance St Village next to the pharmacy. (06) 868 3580.

Around the corner is *Village Antiques and Collectables*, in a bright blue and red cottage at 131 Ormond Rd, next to Health 2000, with whom they share a phone number, (06) 867 0901. They're open most days, 10am to 4.30pm. www.villageantiques.co.nz

There's an *Arthur Toye* store at 75 Gladstone Rd, (06) 867 9619, www.arthurtoye.co.nz. In fact, Gisborne is where it all began — the late Mr Toye set up the first of what would become a chain of fabric businesses in a tiny shop in Gisborne in 1938. And the *Bernina Sewing Centre* at 261 Gladstone Rd is still going after 33 years. A third of their stock is wool and they have a good range of patchwork fabrics too, as well as their sewing machines. Open 9am to 5.30pm weekdays and 9.30am to 1pm Saturday. (06) 867 6835.

While in town, have a look around *Tairawhiti Museum*, where the city's oldest surviving house, the 1872 Wyllie Cottage, still stands out the front. The museum has several significant quilts in its collection; if you're interested, ring well in advance to arrange a viewing. Walk through to the new maritime wing: looking onto the riverbank, it incorporates the restored wheelhouse of the SS *Star of Canada*, wrecked off Kaiti beach in 1912 and for many years a residence on Childers St. If you visited Gisborne in the 1950s, you too were probably taken to see it! Kelvin Rise, Stout St, (06) 867 3832, www.tairawhitimuseum.org.nz

Bodger *Jasper Murphy* has moved out to an organic orchard at Waerengaahika, a 10-minute drive from town. We've followed Jasper's career and have now commissioned two of his exquisite Shaker-style chairs, with woven seagrass seats, for special birthdays. We found his name in the Gisborne Arts and Crafts Trail brochure — free at our motel — and went to watch him working at his foot-powered lathe turning green wood in the traditional English way. Ring first, 235 Harper Rd, (06) 863 0513, www.chairsbyjasper.co.nz

Bushmere Arms, also at Waerengaahika, is a revamped country pub that successfully juggles the needs of local drinkers and fine diners, and features a menu supplied largely from its own organic garden. There's a gorgeous rose garden to wander around, where they do Opera in the Garden from time to time. (06) 862 5820, www.bushmerearms.co.nz

Time to head north along the coast. In the late 1970s, craft collectives once did their spinning, knitting, weaving and pottery in old bank buildings in places like Tokomaru Bay. No longer. There's hardly a town centre left here now. And — let's face it — in summer you'll probably just want to immerse yourself in that unbelievably aqua water.

But don't bypass the *Tolaga Bay Cashmere Company*, housed in an old bank on Solander St, which leads to the beach from the main highway. Although they have boutique stores in Parnell and Christchurch, this is where the world-famous company really began, using the fibre from goats descended from animals that Cook introduced in 1769. The street itself is named after one of Cook's botanists. (06) 862 6746, www.cashmere.co.nz

Off the main road at its southern end, Tolaga Bay has the longest wharf in the southern hemisphere. Built in 1929 to accommodate coastal shipping, it is now succumbing to the ravages of time. It's well worth a stroll for a different perspective on the bay.

You can drive on up around the coast, or take an inland route to connect with Opotiki. We went south instead, leaving Gizzy by Highway 2, the route over the Wharerata Hills, though we have travelled the winding inland Tiniroto route. Highway 2 takes you past the *Morere Hot Springs* north of Nuhaka — definitely worth a stop just to walk around, even if you don't want a dip in the natural waters. Climb gently through nikau-lined paths to the top where the small pools are hottest. Now revamped, they've been open to the public for over a century, like the large mineral pool further down. There's also a cool, open pool at the bottom. You can inspect the craft shop at the entrance without paying the minimal entry fee. Tearooms across the road do a roaring trade, especially on a hot day. (06) 837 8856.

If you take the inland route, you'll find the world-famous *Eastwoodhill Arboretum*, the National Arboretum of New Zealand, well worth a visit. Allow at least a half-day to enjoy some of the 135 hectares of trees. The Friends of Eastwoodhill offer catering but you must order at least five days in advance. You can also stay overnight for a very reasonable price. (06) 863 9003, www.eastwoodhill.org.nz

Mahia Peninsula is another area that's booming, and bound to end up with good craft outlets — but not yet. And Wairoa is still waiting for someone to gently restore some once-grand buildings on its waterfront.

Lake Tutira is well worth a refreshment stop: buy an ice cream from the store and enjoy it at the camping area on the south end. The edge of the revitalised lake, now beautifully landscaped with deciduous trees, has picnic places everywhere.

It's fantastic to hit the coast again at Tangoio, north of Napier, where you can see the art-deco city's Bluff Hill sticking out into the bay.

Art Deco Capital

Central Napier was rebuilt in the newest style after the 1931 earthquake, in which 258 people died and the CBD was razed by fire. The *Art Deco Trust*, 163 Tennyson St, offers a variety of walking and driving trails, including guided tours by volunteers who give a lively introduction to the style before taking to the streets. You can even take tea with deco character Bertie — aka Clarence Bertram St John Fitz Montague — for just the cost of the refreshments, at the historic *Hawke's Bay Club*. (06) 835 0022, www.artdeconapier.com

Much of the city's nightlife takes place around the old inner harbour at Ahuriri, raised by the 1931 earthquake, in an area commonly known as the Iron Pot. Royalty has been seen dining at one of the string of wool stores that have morphed into waterfront bars and restaurants looking across at the Napier Sailing Club's fleet — you can catch a nice sunset here in the winter. My favourite restaurant is *Fox on the Quay* at 14 West Quay. Bookings are essential. (06) 8336520, www.foxonthequay.co.nz

By day, teens will enjoy *Hep Set Mooch* (there's a rock-climbing wall next door) and boomers will laugh at the fifties furnishings. (06) 833 6332.

If you're nostalgic for the days of tea at Grandma's, you'll appreciate *Port O'Call*, in the small shopping centre on Nelson Quay, on the seaward side of the inner harbour. A mix of tea shop and gift shop, it serves tea, coffee, freshly squeezed local juices, and club sandwiches and cake on real china, with floral tablecloths and posies of fresh flowers. You can choose something pretty to take home from their stock of linens, cards, candles and bathroom goodies. (06) 833 6688.

To get back to town you can either pop up Shakespeare Rd and over the hill — note the colourful button mural on a renovated shopfront on the corner as you start to go up — or drive along the waterfront for a more scenic ride. On a good day, grab a coffee at the restaurant behind the fried chicken place — the view is breathtaking. The boardwalk runs from the Iron Pot round to Hardinge Rd, so if you feel you've been sitting in the car too long, take a stroll.

Napier's Tennyson and Hastings Sts are starting to become a hot area of town for shoppers. The *Napier Antique Centre*, on the corner of Tennyson St and Cathedral Lane, has a good stock of textiles among its ranges from different dealers. You'll find good old linen plus vintage clothing here — especially deco-era dress-ups for the annual Art Deco Weekend in February — as well as china, books, paintings, furniture and lots of buttons and jewellery. (06) 835 9865.

Napier's also well off for op shops, both in town and in the suburbs, though not all of them are open every day. Try *St Paul's Presbyterian* op shop in Asher Hall, behind the church in Tennyson St, or the *Cathedral* shop at the hill end of Hastings St.

For stunning jewellery and other work by local craft artists you can't go past *Statements Gallery*, on the corner of Tennyson and Hastings Sts, (06) 834 1331, www.statementsgallery.co.nz

If you hanker after Oriental carpets, Nick Powrie has some gems down the road at *The Magic Carpet* in the Scinde Building, 71 Tennyson St, (06) 8337468, www.themagiccarpet.co.nz

Part exhibition, part design store, part fashion boutique, all style, *Aroha Lamour* took *Urbis* mag's Best Design Store ribbon in 2009. Classy New Zealand designer objects include David Trubridge's wooden furniture and Paula Coulthard's blanket quilts and coats — she co-designed Rattle Your Dags, a World of Wearable Arts winner in 2007. 14 Hastings St, (06) 835 5995, www.houseofaroha.com

There are cafés galore in town, with several good ones within a few strides of the *Bernina Sewing Centre* at 239C Emerson St, (06) 835 8488. *The Olive Branch* at 216 Hastings St has great bread and other goodies.

Hawke's Bay Museum's significant textile collections — including antique quilts and embroideries, 19th-century European settler clothing, art-deco beaded dresses, and accessories through to 1960s New Zealand designer ranges — are packed away until the new building opens in 2013. For updates check www.hbmag.co.nz

One of the most refreshing textile things to happen to Napier in a long time is *Fresh Vintage*, Sue Whitburn's home business on the corner of Carnell Street (number 49) and Georges Drive. She does a great job of remaking old cloth into wearable skirts, bags and cushions in a house featuring the prettiest mural of antique saucers on its garden wall. She also sells vintage china and ephemera, helps run the occasional craft market in Ahuriri, makes an occasional appearance at Craft 2.0 at The Dowse, Lower Hutt, and sells through Craft Country in Featherston. Opening times vary so call (06) 835 6660.

On the way to Taradale — once a borough, but now swallowed up in suburbia — Sue Ward's *Wool 'n' Things* in Maadi Rd, Onekawa, off Kennedy Rd, is still going strong after 20 years. (06) 843 6267.

Not far away in Husheer Place, Onekawa, is family-owned and operated *Skeinz*, the knitters' factory shop, open 10am to 2pm weekdays during summer. They have a yarn club with lots of charity knitting projects — including making jumpers for penguins caught in the Rena oil slick. (06) 843 3174, www.skeinz.com

Jan Gilray's *JJ's Crafts Ltd* — now relocated to 14 Gloucester St, Greenmeadows (the main road), opposite the huge New World store — began life in a wool store as a hand-dyed knitting yarn business. Jan has now sold that but still stocks brilliant coloured wools, embroidery threads from around the world, beads, ribbons and patchwork fabrics. She and her team do mail order and are open seven days. (06) 844 0680, www.jjscrafts.co.nz

On the main road, just before Taradale's war memorial clock tower, you'll find the op shop behind *St Columba's Presbyterian Church*. It's open Tuesday to Thursday and good for fossicking. Taradale itself is a pleasant place to poke around — there are good clothing boutiques, florists and gift shops. It is also the home of multi-award-winning knitwear designer, fibre artist and teacher *Laurel Judd* — look out for her sign at 32 Trigg Cres. Call first on (06) 844 8621, www.laurel.co.nz

Out at Puketapu — on the very road where I first plucked sheep's wool off the fences to make dollies' quilts — is *Patch and Quilt*, where registered nurse and sociology graduate Rachel Cadwallader's shop and classroom share a barn at her home with Riverside Wines. It's worth going out there just for the drive from Taradale or Hastings through the beautiful Hawke's Bay countryside — and you can buy wine too. Non-crafty companions can make themselves comfortable on one of the couches with a cuppa. Rachel also welcomes quilters who are passing through and have time to spare, with a machine available for their use. Long-arm quilter Lesley O'Rourke of *Quarryburn Quilting*, 0800 434 796, has a room through the shop. It's just 10 minutes from Taradale, 20 minutes from Napier or Hastings. 434 Dartmoor Rd, (06) 844 4942, www.patchandquilt.co.nz. Some of Rachel's customers stay across the road in a vineyard at *Cover Point Cottage*, which has a minimum two-night stay and provides breakfast. (06) 844 4336.

Sherelyn Whiteman's *Heirlooms* is located in her home, Wyndom House, a relocated and restored villa on Pakowhai Road, halfway between Napier and Hastings. She has a marvellous mix of threads, ribbons, beads, patterns and fabrics for embroidery, all in an Aladdin's cave of a front room. She does morning teas for groups, who come by the busload. Just before the bridge on the western side of the Tutaekuri River — opposite Copperfields Antiques and next to Orcona Chillis. Sherelyn also publishes patterns under her label Barberry Row. Open Fridays 10am to 4pm, including PT — Peace and Tranquillity — sessions when you're welcome to meet up with friends, drop in with your own project, or simply call in for coffee — or by appointment. On the last Thursday of each month there is a Natter night — 'Needle And Thread Together Equals Relaxation' — from 6.30pm. 1821 Pakowhai Rd, RD3, Napier, 0800 588 978

Hastings is responding to Napier's art-deco tourist boom with an emphasis on its own Spanish Mission architecture, boasting some fine examples of the style that originated in southern California.

On your way into town you absolutely must stop for a cone at the famous *Rush Munro's Ice Cream Gardens*. Established just days after the 1931 quake, the business — in a setting complete with goldfish pond and green trellis garden room — has been at 704 Heretaunga St ever since. The ice cream, still made to the original recipe, is now sold round the country — but there's nothing quite like licking a feijoa or malted milk cone, in the traditional pyramid shape, right where it all started. Open every day but hours restricted in winter. (06) 878 9634, www.rushmunro.co.nz

Knit World is at 322 Heretaunga St West, (06) 878 0090, and *Spotlight*, with its usual range of goodies, is on the corner of Avenue Rd and Market St — one of a burgeoning number of big-box developments around the CBD. (06) 878 5223.

Jo Pearson and Jess Soutar Barron, the crafters behind *Fruit Bowl Craft Jam*, held at the Hawke's Bay Opera House, now have an open workroom and sometime shop. *Coco and Co* — open Fridays, Saturdays or by arrangement, at 106 Market St — has grown out of a combined passion for 'hand-made, design-led, found, upcycled and recycled objects — the beautiful, the useful, the interesting, the obscure, the nostalgic and sometimes, given the right light, the grotesque'. The latter, of course, refers to the lampshades they pair with found bases to create one-off conversation pieces, along with fun cushions and pouffes. Jo's jewellery — she taught at the inaugural Handmade symposium — combines the weird and the wonderful. 021 217 0601, www.cocoandco.co.nz

Also in Hastings on the main street is Donald Hurley's *Hastings Rubber Stamps*, which specialises in everything scrapbookers need. 416 West Heretaunga St, (06) 876 4865, www.hasrub.co.nz

 I love *White Traders Secondhand Dealers*, (06) 879 5290, opposite the Omahu Rd Caltex Station on the western outskirts of Hastings. They often have textile bits and pieces among the cartons of crockery and other stuff rounded up at auctions in the capital. I nabbed myself three turquoise linen napkins this trip, along with a couple of $4 clothes brushes — brand new! They'll negotiate on prices if you're buying a bundle — in short, they're definitely worth a visit. There's parking off the busy road. For a leafy treat, drive down nearby Oak Avenue. They'll tell you how to find it.

 Havelock North is another village that's been almost swallowed up in suburbia. Among the great shops is the original *Redcurrent* store; (06) 877 6770. Havelock has some charming shops, including *Clothesline* fashion boutique and *Bedside Manor*, both on Joll Rd, where you can buy readymade quilts. (06) 877 4455.

 Up the road, past the supermarket entrance, is the *Presbyterian op shop* — I've bought more than half a dozen Liberty blouses here over the years, perhaps a reflection of the village's gentility. And on Friday mornings the *St Luke's Anglican op shop* around on Te Mata Rd is open for business.

 Jackson's on Joll — a branch of the award-winning bakery around the corner — and *Hawthorne Coffee Roasters'* base down in Napier Rd are good for coffee and lunch.

If you love Liberty fabric, chances are you'll already have come across *Christabel Liberty Dress Fabric*. Christabel Tylee used to operate down on the farm in central Hawke's Bay before she and her husband Richard moved to 86 Kopanga Rd, Havelock North. Here, a room over the garage behind their restored 1906 house, overlooking the Heretaunga Plains, showcases their 200-plus Liberty fabrics and shirts, nightdresses and hats. Please ring first.
(06) 877 6220, www.christabels.co.nz

Havelock North's arty and crafty people have one of the best settings anywhere in which to spin, knit, paint and stitch, at a heritage house behind the town. Originally part of the Chambers family's Tauroa Station, the park-like *Keirunga Gardens* at 5 Kopanga Road was given to the people of Havelock North in 1956 by George Nelson, who was inspired in his planting by London's Kew Gardens. The groups comprising the Keirunga Arts & Crafts Society meet in various areas of the old homestead — spinners in the house, miniaturists in the laundry, painters and potters in a purpose-built studio and exhibition space out the back. Keirunga Quilters meet in the Quilters' Cottage in the garden. If you're visiting, drive in — you might be lucky.

There's a special place to spend a night or two in Havelock North. Margaret and David Cranwell's two-bedroom retreat at 35 *River Rd* was built for family and every detail is beautifully thought through. It gets all-day sun, and looks out over vineyards to a riverbank trail, well-used by walkers and cyclists. In autumn there's golden colour on the vineyards below. The house is filled with New Zealand art — Margaret was a gallery director in Hastings — and with its enclosed paved courtyard outside would make a fabulous venue for a small wedding. (06) 877 5299, www.35riverroad.co.nz

If I'm doing a day trip out of Napier I always stop at *Hohepa Cheesery*, just south of the second bridge on the way to the little township of Clive, for organic cheese and yoghurt. They make a Danbo style — with or without cumin seeds — mozzarella and feta, plus fresh ricotta and quark, which also comes in herbed or lemon and honey versions. (06) 870 0426, www.hohepa.com/hawkes-bay-the-cheesery.php

It's worth stopping in the bustling country town of Waipukurau for Clare Moore's *Quilt Works*, signposted off the bypass through the thriving central Hawke's Bay town. From a room in the front of her house in a suburban Waipukurau street, she has recently graduated to a purpose-built shop that includes a classroom. Husband Kerry looks after the Janome machines — the couple went to the international conference in Orlando, Florida, along with half a dozen other Kiwi Janome stockists. Clare loves visits by groups and will arrange morning teas if asked. 8 Marlborough St, (06) 858 9280, www.quiltworks.co.nz

Dannevirke has lost some of its better shops, unfortunately. The remaining antique business is *Charlesfort Antiques*, on the main street, next to the BNZ. I was delighted to find some walkie-talkie dolls just like the ones we had as kids — they came complete with clothes, too — the only ones I saw on this trip. Open 10am to 5pm most days. 027 447 0008.

Across the road is a *St Vincent de Paul* op shop which closes at 3pm sharp, as I've occasionally found to my disappointment. There's invariably something here to take home; this time it was a pair of smocked Viyella dresses in autumn colours — what a find! I left several matching pairs of tartan skirts on bodices in the shop, but the 'best dresses', which surely belonged to twin redheads, maybe eight years old, were irresistible.

Woodville, technically part of Manawatu, is covered in the next chapter.

Baby Coat-Hanger Covers

Use bits of leftover yarn to knit up little coat-hanger covers in a flash and have fun embellishing them with your favourite ribbon or buttons. Not only do they add charm to a baby's room, but they also keep tiny clothes from slipping off the hanger. They make a lovely last-minute gift idea for a baby shower too.

MATERIALS

Balls of leftover worsted or DK-weight yarn
5.5 mm (US 9) straight needles
Plain 30 cm (12") wooden hangers (available in craft stores)
Bits of ribbon or buttons for decoration
Yarn needle for finishing
Needle and thread to match yarn or decorations
Tension is not important for this pattern

DESIGNED BY: HADLEY FIERLINGER, VINTAGE KNITS FOR MODERN BABIES

DIRECTIONS

Tip: You knit the hanger cover as a long, narrow rectangle just
a bit shorter than your hanger length, because the cover can be
stretched to fit snugly when you stitch it together at the bottom.
Poke the metal hook back through the middle of the rectangle
before stitching.

With 2 strands of yarn together, cast on 9 sts, and work in garter
stitch until work measures 23 cm (9"). Cast off, leaving a 30 cm (12")
tail for sewing together.

Poke the hanger's metal hook through the middle of the cover,
so that knitting lies along the top of the hanger. Using the yarn
tail, sew the side and bottom edges together, using mattress stitch
or whipstitch.

Tuck in the loose ends as you go. Embellish with buttons or ribbon
as desired.

Chapter Five

TARANAKI
AND MANAWATU

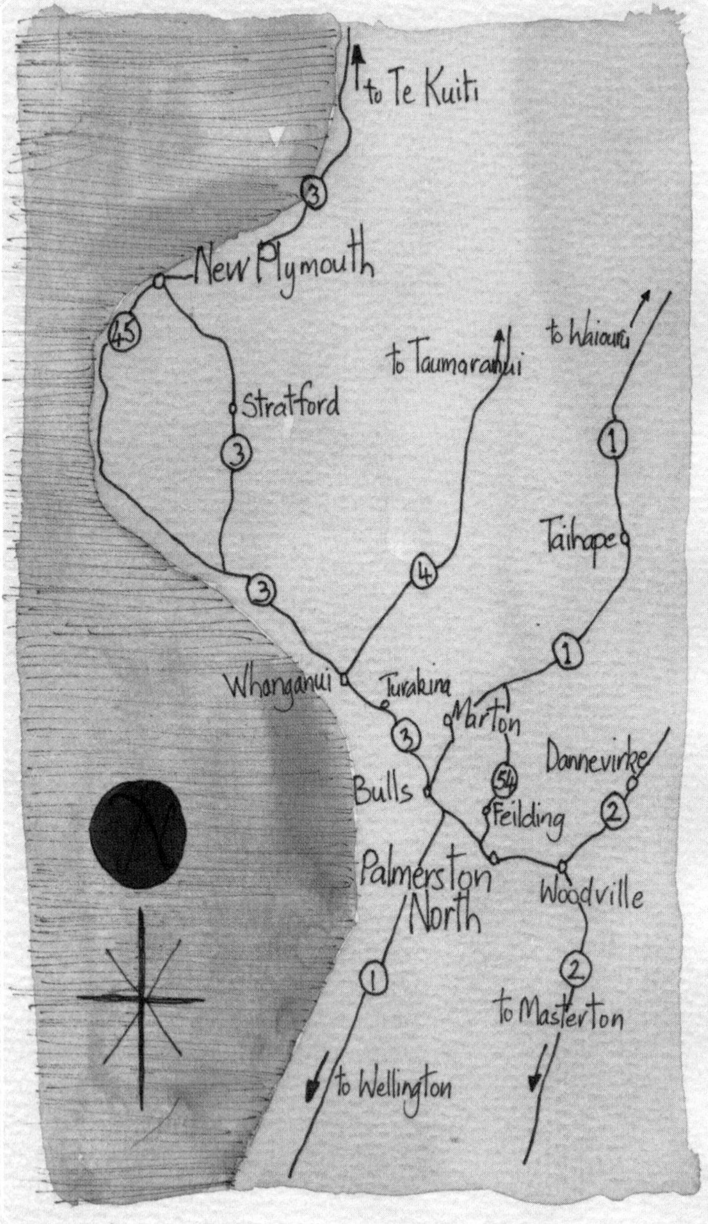

to Te Kuiti
3
New Plymouth
45
Stratford
3
to Taumarunui
to Waiouru
1
Taihape
4
3
1
Whanganui
Turakina
Marton
3
54
Dannevirke
Bulls
Feilding
2
Palmerston North
Woodville
1
2
to Masterton
to Wellington

This trip we were caught out in a deluge that surprised even the most hardened of this lush province's dairy farmers. When we turned up the driveway of our Stratford B&B it was raining so hard we couldn't even contemplate getting out of the car.

But next morning, against all expectations, the bad weather lifted — enough blue sky to make a sailor a pair of pyjamas, as Nana used to say, but not enough to see the mountain itself. We came into the coastal city of New Plymouth once again to a vision of the sea, rolling in to shore straight across the road from the CBD, with Len Lye's stunning 45-metre *Wind Wand* waving a welcome.

We'd stayed the night at the grand old two-storeyed *Hathaway House* — no, not named after the Shakespeare connection — as the thunder and lightning raged outside. Relieved that we had decided to stop short of New Plymouth, we finally took shelter inside — a warm fire, curtains pulled and we were safe at last. Just past the Stratford town boundary. 3500 Mountain Rd, (06) 765 4189, hathawayhouse.co.nz

New Plymouth has come alive with the completion of *Puke Ariki*, the museum and information centre that's linked across the road to the library. Open seven days; entry is free. (06) 759 6060, pukeariki.com. There's parking beneath the building and you have the choice of two cafés. The one in the library wing serves casual food like muffins to go with your coffee. Otherwise you can have a coffee at the upmarket *Arborio*, which has the very best view of the bay, and serves meals from breakfast through to dinner. We soaked up the seascape from the verandah, sharing the view and lattes with a couple of rugby tourists. The ugly multi-storeyed carpark across the rolling lawn still obscures what should be a spectacular coastal vista. St Aubyn St, (06) 759 1241.

If you want salt-laden sea air but find the four-lane highway a bit daunting, there's an underpass to get to Puke Ariki, across on the waterfront path. If you've time, you can walk the whole 7 km from Port Taranaki to Lake Rotomanu, which includes the spectacularly sculptural Te Rewa Rewa pedestrian bridge over the Waiwhakaiho River.

Just a block away from Puke Ariki is the *Govett-Brewster Art Gallery* in Queen St, with its collection of contemporary New Zealand and Pacific Rim works, a branch of the NZ Film Archive and the Len Lye

Archive — as well as its current exhibitions. They also have a café, which is open 8am to 5pm daily. (06) 759 6060, www.govettbrewster.com

You should be aware that New Plymouth has a one-way street system operating in part of the CBD, so going around the block looking for parks can be tricky for visitors. There are quite a few parking areas dotted around, but street parking is available too.

It's worth dropping in to *St Mary's* Anglican pro-cathedral, four blocks up from the water, simply for the breathtaking stillness in the sanctuary. Volunteers will proudly show you around New Zealand's oldest stone church, built in 1846 of beach stones that seem to retain the smell of the ocean. It's home to an impressive collection of regimental flags and ecclesiastical embroidery, including the historic St Mary Banner, created in 1907–08, refurbished in 1955 and restored again in 2003. The latest embroidered work is a Peace Altar Frontal, worked on by volunteers and visitors alike, and dedicated on 6 November 2011, the day the church remembers peacemaker Te Whiti o Rongomai. Open daily. 37 Vivian St, (06) 758 3111.

Taranaki's only specialist patchwork and quilting store takes its name from founder Glenys Still. Robyn Hendry and Leanne Munro are now the owners of *Still Quilting & Knitting* at 228 Devon St East, New Plymouth's main street. They have a large stock of fabrics, including flannels — well, you'd need them, under that mountain. The wool room has plenty to lure knitters, including exclusive patterns from young American guru — and choreographer — Stephen West, with enough samples to entice you into buying at least one ball to knit one of his fine shawls. (06) 758 6255, stillquiltingndknitting.blogspot.com

Also on Devon St East are *Knit World*, at number 129, (06) 758 3171, and the *Bernina Sewing Centre* at number 37, (06) 758 3268. There's a *Spotlight* store at 139 Gill St, not far from Puke Ariki. Open seven days, (06) 757 3575.

Last trip I found a big stash of vintage clothing and yardage at Andy King and Leonie Keys' *Chadz Collectables* at 50 Liardet St. Andy says that wasn't moving very much so if that's what you want, ring in advance! (06) 758 4966, a/h (06) 758 4966. Open weekdays and Saturday mornings from 'about 10.30'. Next door is the *Methodist op shop*, which has new knitted goodies including hottie bottle covers.

There are design stores aplenty in New Plymouth too. For New Zealand objects try *Kina*, in the venerable 1894 wooden Exchange Chambers building at 101 Devon St West, just around the corner from the Govett-Brewster Art Gallery. Lots of textiles here: Seam blanket cushions, flax kete and hapene (stripped flax) work, plus dolls by Dunedin artist Juliet Novena Sorrel. (06) 759 1201, www.kina.co.nz

A really special place to stay in New Plymouth is the refurbished 140-year-old *Nice Hotel*, 71 Brougham St. A boutique establishment in the heart of town, it's had rave reviews from all quarters. It has just six suites but offers the luxuries that go with a big hotel — good artwork, in-house dining — while maintaining the personal service of a small one. You can see Len Lye's *Wind Wand* from here, and walk to the Govett-Brewster, Puke Ariki and St Mary's church. If you don't need overnight accommodation, you can still eat in the bistro. Nice one! (06) 758 6423, www.nicehotel.co.nz

If you've time and it's a nice day the drive out to Oakura takes around 20 minutes — check out the surf, shop for souvenirs in John Sole and Tony Barnes' *The Crafty Fox* (open seven days in an old church) and eat in a genuine vintage railway carriage behind it. The *Carriage Café* will come up with something to suit your appetite even if it's not on the menu; (06) 752 7226. John and Tony also have a garden to visit by arrangement. (06) 752 7873, www.ngamamakugarden.co.nz

Going the inland way means stopping in Inglewood for coffee at local icon *Macfarlane's Caffe*, in their restored building on the corner of Kelly and Matai Sts — you can't miss it. Open 9am to 5pm seven days a week. (06) 756 6665. There are several good op shops in Inglewood, all easy to spot from the main route, but the biggest drawcard for those who fondly remember their sandpit days is the *FunHo National Toy Museum*, with over 3000 toys on display. Open seven days. (06) 756 7030, www.funhotoys.co.nz

Back through Stratford, without the rain, we call in at Maudette Brown's *In Stitches* store at 200 Broadway, the main street, (06) 765 4164. It's been here forever — Hathaway House's Lisa Gilmer, who made my delicious French toast for breakfast, remembers it from her childhood — and Maudette has worked here much longer than she's owned the business. She calls it an old-fashioned store — she even has hooks for the form of crochet known variously as Afghan, Tunisian or Tricot. As well as stocking a big range of patchwork and dressmaking fabrics, wool and notions of every kind, In Stitches is known for knitted and stitched samples available at great prices. *Nelson's Bakery* is next door.

Eltham is becoming something of a destination for Taranaki shoppers. There are enough retro and second-hand dealers to make a trip worthwhile, plus a couple of cafés too. On the main road at 160 High St is *Antiques & Effects*, a china shop of the old-fashioned kind, open seven days. (06) 764 8860. Across the road is a very different kettle of fish. *Fortyseven* is full of good stuff but owner Miss Paisley's life is up in the air at present — 'I'm more famous for being closed' — which happens when you have a couple of gorgeous young sons to raise and your mum is ill. Fortyseven is, as Miss Paisley says, full of possibilities but they may be more virtual than real for a while. Take your chances. (06) 764 8978, www.fortysevenonlinestore.com

You can bank on finding vintage riches around the corner at Barbara Valintine's eclectic store *The Bank*, in a gloriously restored old bank building she fell in love with four years ago. I found capacious old knitting bags and there were some good old crocheted afghans. Closed Mondays or view by appointment. 51 Bridge St, (06) 764 7452, www.thebank.net.nz

Across the street is Heather Fyfe's textile treasure trove, *Decodently Yours*. It's full of immaculately presented scarves, aprons, blankets and clothing as well as jewellery. It's closed Sundays and Mondays but you can text to arrange a visit. 88 Bridge St, 027 348 9032.

Back in the main street, Cambodian-born Meng makes a good cup of coffee at her *Inflame Café*, open every day. 139 High St, (06) 764 8272.

On the edge of the Hawera bypass, Ngaire Low's 30-year business *Ethel Anne Antiques* offered rich pickings for this fossicker — if I'd had more cash I might have bought all the simple, vari-sized cloth bags embroidered with the initials RBL; as it was, I opted for one, which had surely been a shoe bag. It's thought they were from a member of the Lysaght family, who 'travelled a lot overseas'. Ethel Anne also has a good selection of nursery china, something I seem to be collecting quite a bit of since I became a grandmother. Cnr Princes St and South Rd, (06) 278 7238.

At Waverley we had to make a pit stop at *The Big Sun Café* on the main road, Weraroa Rd, for one of Helen Beaurepaire's legendary custard squares. Open seven days. (06) 346 5511.

Whanganui — the River City

What's happened to all Whanganui's legendary junk shops? Renovators used to travel from Wellington for recycled architectural salvage like windows, flooring and fireplaces, but of the shops, *Antiques & Elegant Junk* has gone, as has *Top Hat*.

Sarah Brierley's *Victoria's Treasures*, at 42 Victoria Ave — the main street running up from the bridge — has antiques, collectables and gifts including 'pretties' from local dollmaker Jill Maas, better known for her character dolls and as a dollmaking teacher. (06) 347 7794. Around in Guyton St at number 70A is Rob and Camilla Leask's *Curiosity*, selling old books, antiques and collectables, including some lovely china.

Across the road at 19 Victoria Ave is compulsory coffee stop *Jolt* — good Ripe coffee in the 1864 Drews Building. *Element,* in the splendid old 1906 BNZ building, is an upmarket lunch stop — it was the entertainment venue for the world premiere of the movie *River Queen,* which screened two doors away at the Embassy Theatre. 26 Victoria St, (06) 345 7028, www.elementcafe.co.nz

Affordable Blinds and Curtains Direct is at 136 Victoria Ave, (06) 348 8474, and at 165 Victoria Ave is the *Wanganui Home Sewing Centre.* Don't be misled by the main street window display, which tends to emphasise the sewing machine part of the business — their patchwork fabric is hidden at the back of the shop. Jeanette and Owen Holdaway also stock dress fabrics and patterns, gorgeous ribbons, embroidery threads, fabrics and kits, plus a huge range of haberdashery. They sell Janome machines and overlockers, and also repair machines. (06) 345 2299.

There's a *Woolmart* at 96 Victoria Ave, and the intriguingly named *Garney Spooner Knitters Wool Shop* at 93 Guyton St is open from 7.30am (yes, it's true) to 5pm weekdays and 9.30am to noon Saturdays. (06) 345 3308.

The local *Save the Children Fund* shop at 176 Victoria Ave has knitters who come up with some lovely — and cheap — knitteds for babies, plus tea cosies and super old-fashioned hottie covers for winter. (06) 348 8407. Two doors away is the *Hospice Boutique* — a bit too boutiquey for me but check it out; 172 Victoria Ave. There's also a big *Sallies* op shop at 299 Victoria Ave, on the corner of Dublin St. (06) 345 2779.

Be sure to drive to the top of Queen's Park at Cameron Tce and see what's on at the stunning *Sarjeant Gallery*, with its central dome, designed by Christchurch architect Samuel Hurst Seager. The building, overlooking the centre of the city, was opened in 1919; current remodelling is reconnecting the gallery with the main street. Plenty of parking here, and a small bookshop. (06) 349 0506.

Open again under new ownership is *Turakina Antiques and Collectables*, in the old chenille factory on the main road south at Turakina. Former Turakina girl Shona Welsh and her husband Ian plan to open a café at some stage and would like to let the antiques shop. Closed Thursdays. (06) 327 3617.

Bulls is the crossroads with Highway 1 where everything has the town's name incorporated in a punny title. Many a night-time traveller, heading north, has missed the turning to Taihape and shot through to Whanganui by mistake. There are several antique shops here, as well as the retail outlet for Rangitikei lavender growers *Scullys*, so step inside and be overwhelmed by natural fragrance. 104 Bridge St (the main road), (06) 322 1838.

We turned into Foxton this trip and found some good reasons to stop. We bought flour stone-ground at the 2003 replica windmill *Die Molen*, where for a small fee you can take a self-guided tour. (06) 363 5601. And I can confirm that Adele Parson's 'famous lemon meringue pie' — made every day from local fruit at her *Tram Station Café* — deserves every accolade; it doesn't get much better than this piled-high meringue and mouth-puckering lemon goodness. We also loved her memorial to New Zealand's 28th Maori Battalion, of which her great-uncle Bgdr George Dittmer was one of the original four Pakeha officers. 100 Main St, (06) 363 8940. Foxton also has a *Flax Stripper Museum*, behind the mill — a working exhibit initiated by botanist David Bellamy when he heard there was no memorial to the early colonial industry of rope making. Locals took him up on it in 1990. Open 1–3pm daily except Christmas Day, Good Friday and Anzac Day. (06) 363 6846. There's also an historical museum in the old courthouse.

Also in Foxton at 16 Main St is a fossicking place going by the splendid name of *Goldies Junk 'N Disorderly* — motto: 'We buy junk and sell antiques'. (06) 363 6950.

Further up the line at Taihape, the place to stop is *Brown Sugar Café* on Huia St, with fabulous home-baked food (including Danish pastries) and good coffee, a garden courtyard if it's fine and a potbelly stove if it's not. Oh, and stacks of magazines plus some tempting gifts. (06) 388 1880.

It's worth taking time to stroll round Taihape ('Gumboot Capital of the World'), which has quite a few shops that reward exploring — casual and outdoor clothing, gifts, and a Levi's seconds shop — and a huge Jeff Thomson corrugated-iron gumboot sculpture.

Just a block away from Brown Sugar is Pauline Baddeley's shop *The Quilted Gumboot*, which sells fabric, thread, wool and patterns. 6 Tui St, (06) 388 1731.

South of Taihape, at Utiku, is the *The Wool Company*, in Torea St, just off Highway 1. It sells gorgeous soft-pastel felted scarves, along with jerseys and other garments, merino, Corriedale and Perendale fleeces, natural-coloured and dyed carded sliver, and hand-knitting and weaving yarns. Open weekdays 8.30am to 5pm, Saturdays 10am to 1pm. 0800 607 010, www.thewoolcompany.com

 Heading south again, Anna Gratton's *Little Wool Company* out of Feilding has supplied fleece, carded wool, knitting and weaving yarns to spinners, weavers and hand and machine knitters for 30 years. She sells her chunky and fine wool, mohair, synthetic and silk fibres in natural or rainbow colours — as well as buttons, patterns and needles — by mail order, on the internet and at some of Dunkley's Craft Shows. But you can also visit her farm shop at Williamson Rd, Waituna West, by arrangement. It's a good chance to choose one of her kits of mixed-colour bouclé and plain wool, with a pattern ready to go. Get clicking! (06) 328 6868, www.annagratton.co.nz

 B B French Antiques, formerly known as the Sanson Antique Centre, on the Palmerston North side of the crossroads where the Palmy road meets Highway 1, is well worth a visit. The shop, which has the feel of a design store, stocks china, ceramics, glass and other more rustic country collectables. Closed Tuesdays, Wednesdays. (06) 329 3467.

Crafty in Palmy

Palmerston North was at the forefront of the New Zealand quilt renaissance at the end of the seventies. It still has two specialist quilt shops, plus an Arthur Toye fabric store with a big craft range, a Bernina shop and a Morelands store. And there are still plenty of op shops and vintage stores to check out in this university town.

Canny crafters can pick up some dazzling bargains in Liberty fabrics, vintage costume and recyclable textiles. The Methodist church has a hierarchy of goodwill shops, with the largest, *Wesley Vintage*, in King St. Longtime practitioner of all things crafty, Merlin Sampson is one of the volunteers behind the scenes at *Arohanui Hospice Shop*, on Rangitikei St. The veteran quilter, miniaturist, spinner (again) and teacher screens incoming donations for the annual Vintage Fair — she's come across everything from a live hand grenade to a coffin but really treasures the occasional fine china find as well as textiles, which she also screens at the Methodist shop for their annual linens fair. 285 Rangitikei St, (06) 356 1960.

Diane Jochem had a collectables shop in Broadway for many years and considered herself retired when she sold the building. But she can't resist old stuff so she's popped up again in a huge and delightful premises further west along Rangatikei St from the Hospice shop, on the road to Whanganui. Allow a good half-hour ... at least. 495 Rangatikei Line (06) 358 5750.

You'll find the Palmerston North branch of good old fabric shop *Arthur Toye* at 191-194 The Square; (06) 357 0345, www.arthurtoyefabrics.co.nz. Next door, at 196 The Square, is knitting chain *Knit World*, (06) 356 8974, www.knitting.co.nz. Also nearby is *Moreland Fabrics* at 517A Main St, (07) 354 8678.

Bernina owners will enjoy the club nights every second month at *Bernina Sewing Centre*, cnr Main St and Victoria Ave, (06) 356 7053.

The Cloth Shop at 48 Victoria Ave was set up by a couple of quilting friends who liked to design their own quilts, cushions and bags. The shop is not big but it's always busy, with a classroom out the back and stock arranged to tempt you into small spaces to look carefully. Katherine Gough, now the sole owner, keeps in touch with customers via a free newsletter that includes lots of personal detail, so you feel you're meeting up with quilting friends. Despite being into her 12th year in the business, Katherine says she still gets that feeling of 'going all goosepimply' just opening a box of fabric and seeing what's inside. For $2 you can roll up on a Friday to get together with other quilters and stitch your current project. There are lots of classes in the shop during evenings and weekends; casual customers benefit too — if the lights are on, says Katherine, 'consider us open'. Husqvarna dealers. (06) 358 1196, www.clothshop.co.nz

Dianne Southey started her *Village Books and Crafts* business as a bookshop at Hokowhitu in 1984, adding fabric three years later — which makes her one of the longest survivors in the quilt supplies trade. She now operates out of a studio at 318 College St, where she's at home Tuesday to Friday 10am to 4pm and Saturdays 10am to 1pm or by appointment. She offers Sit and Sew-cial nights every Thursday. (06) 355 5735, villagebooksandcrafts.blogspot.com

Vallis and Lyn Peet reluctantly closed *Needlecraft Distributors'* doors in September 2011 when Vallis turned 70. After 30 years in business, which included selling penguin fabric to a settlement near the North Pole, they're now web-only, dealing in magazines and books — 'things that don't take up too much room!', www.needlecraft.co.nz

If I'm heading up towards Hawke's Bay I like to stop further up the line at Woodville, where there are half a dozen shops catering for those who like resuscitating old treasures. Within two small blocks you can find everything from antiques to tat — and most are open seven days. My favourite is the Ashwell family-owned *Woodville Mart*, (06) 376 5865, in an old picture theatre: special buys here have included a canvas deckchair, vintage tools (oiled but not tarted up to disguise any flaws) and fifties-era travel bags. *Village Traders Woodville*, (06) 376 4446, also has a mix of old tools and household stuff. *Whariti Antiques*, (06) 376 5595, specialises in glorious antique furniture and whole dinner services. There is also a motley collection of second-hand shops filling up empty premises — who knows if they will last.

Around in the old Country Women's Institute building is Evan Nattrass' aptly named *Viking's Haul*. A longtime collector of almost everything strange and sometimes useful, he's stashed it all into his hall on the corner of Ross and Pollen Sts, opposite the town's good public toilets. Opening hours unpredictable. (06) 376 5553.

On the corner of the main road, Vogel St, and Ross St is Tracy White's *Inspire Fibres*, where the seasoned textile artist turns wool, alpaca and silk into rainbow-hued slivers for spinners, knitters, weavers, felters and silk papermakers. Her fibre studio in the old mailroom of the former Woodville post office is next door to the police station. (06) 376 5155, tracywhite@inspire.net.nz

The fish and chip shop on the main street just before the turn-off to the Wairarapa is always chocker when we stop — but don't let the wait put you off: their shark and taties are mouthwatering. Like many other local businesses, they've suffered from the prolonged closure of the Manawatu Gorge since major slips occurred in the spring of 2011.

Dannevirke, further north, has some good old stuff. It's covered in the East Coast of the North Island chapter.

Journal Cover

REQUIREMENTS
Medium weight woven fabric recommended.

FABRIC DIMENSIONS
Height of diary + 30 mm (15 mm seam allowance top and bottom).
Width of diary x 2 (front & back) + spine width + 200 mm (this gives
a 90 mm pocket on the inside covers — this could be increased or
decreased depending on the size of the diary — i.e. if narrower,
decrease the pocket allowance).

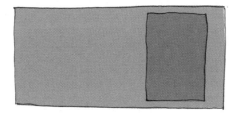

DESIGNED BY: GENEVIEVE PACKER, WELLINGTON

INSTRUCTIONS

1. Cut out cloth.
2. Fold in a 10 mm seam allowance at either end, pressing it towards the wrong side. Stitch down.

3. Turn the fabric right side up and fold over 90 mm at one end towards the right side. Stitch top and bottom 15 mm in from each edge.

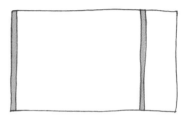

4. Insert one end of the diary to check the fit — it should sit nice and tight. It it's too loose, increase the seam allowance till it's snug.

5. With the diary sitting snug in the sewn end, wrap fabric around the diary and close it. Mark the end point of the diary cover on the fabric with chalk or a pin.
6. Remove the diary, fold the end over at the marked point, press and sew as per the first end.
7. Insert the diary to check the fit.

8. While the cover is inside out, fold down the visible raw edges top and bottom between the sewn pockets, extending 15 mm beyond the sewn pocket line. Stitch, but be careful to catch only this piece of cloth, not the seam allowance behind.

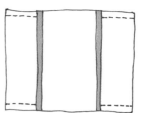

9. Fold these edges down to sit flush with the sewn pocket lines, tapering up to full height before the fold of the pocket.

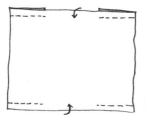 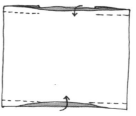

10. Bag out — poke the corners out with a knitting needle if necessary.
11. Slip the diary in — it may be easier to bend the diary cover backwards to do this.
12. Separating the two layers of seams to sit either side of the cover, although fiddly, makes for a nicer finish.

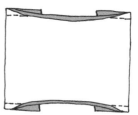

Chapter Six

WELLINGTON AND
WAIRARAPA

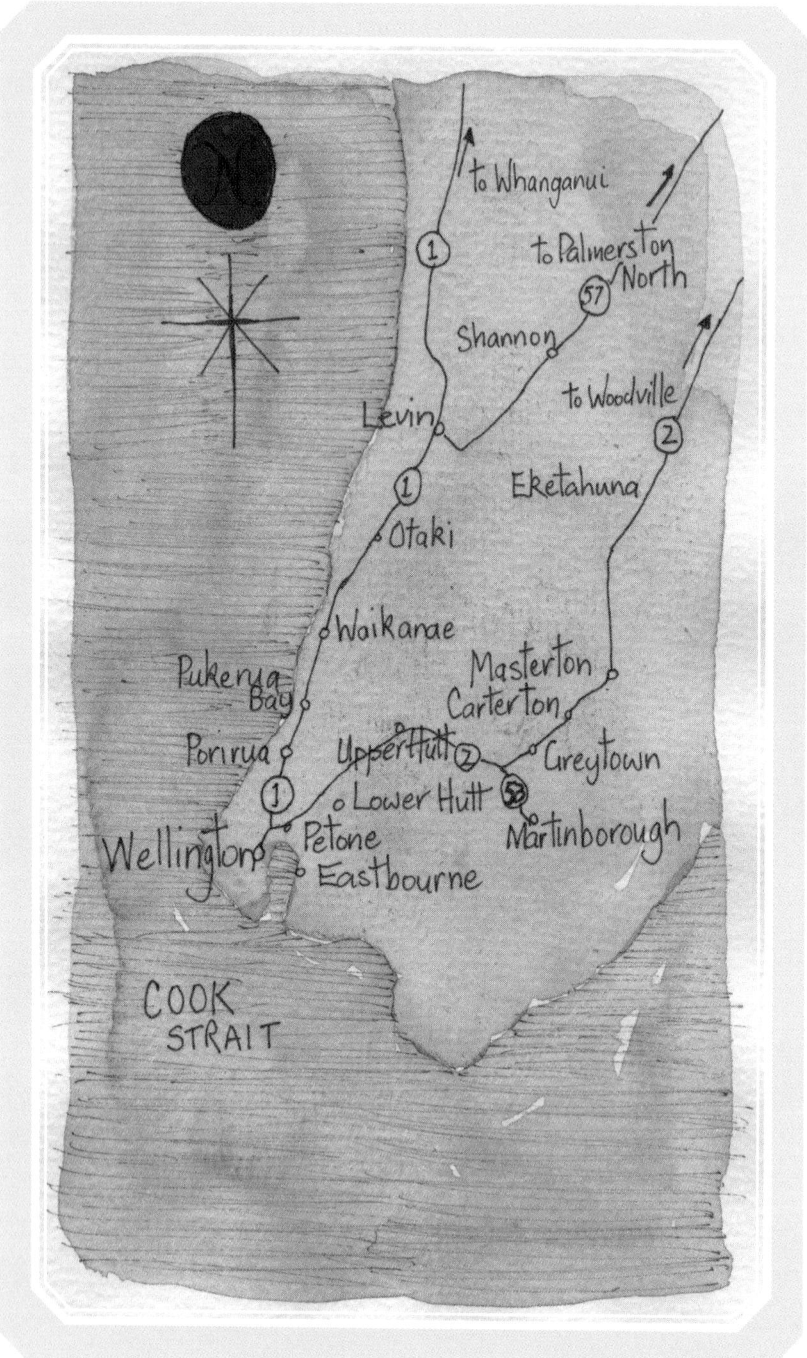
N
to Whanganui
1
to Palmerston North
57
Shannon
to Woodville
Levin
2
1
Eketahuna
Otaki
Waikanae
Masterton
Pukerua Bay
Carterton
Porirua
Upper Hutt
2
Greytown
1
Lower Hutt
53
Petone
Martinborough
Wellington
Eastbourne
COOK STRAIT

Wellington may well be the seat of government but for many who live here it's the cultural and creative richness of the capital city that really matters.

Mary Self, owner of Nancys Embroidery, notes there are now three annual textile events in Wellington — the *World of Wearable Arts (WOW)*, which came across from Nelson in 2005; *Handmade*, the celebration of all things crafty at Queen's Birthday weekend, which took off in 2011, and — believe it or not — the annual Rugby Sevens tournament. Mary says hotels even ring her wanting to hire sewing machines for fans who have arrived without costumes!

The city centre is compact enough to get around easily, either on foot or by bus. And there's a ferry option if you're visiting Eastbourne, across the harbour.

Among the region's textile drawcards are some very public artworks, a specialist textile gallery and bookshop, a public gallery committed to applied arts and a perfect gem of a pioneer cottage. There are also works in public collections which can be viewed by appointment.

If you're looking for a special place to stay, Jane Tolerton's *Booklovers Bed and Breakfast*, on Mt Victoria near the green belt, offers 'the greatest comfort with the least fuss, my motto being "I'd rather be reading"'. You can hire her whole renovated late-Victorian house with its ensuite bathrooms, or just a single room. There are, of course, lots of books, and you're within 15 minutes' walk of restaurants and theatres on Courtenay Place, Te Papa and the Museum of Wellington City and Sea along the waterfront. 123 Pirie St, (04) 384 2714, www.booklovers.co.nz

Another book-rich B&B on the other side of town is textile-rich too. Bernice Ryan's French-styled boutique *The Bay Window*, at 200 Tinakori Rd, is perfectly situated to make browsing Thorndon's shops a breeze. An antiques dealer who recently returned to the capital after seven years in Auckland's Birkenhead, Bernice has a love of all things French which shows in her beautifully appointed home — a 1900 bay villa originally built for the Thorndon constable — as well as in her Thorndon village shop, which she walks to each day with her West Highland white terrier, Maxie. (See *Vintage Antiques* on page 135) (04) 499 0345, www.thebaywindow.co.nz

Astoria, opening onto Midland Park on Lambton Quay, is my town office — a large café where you get your coffee quickly at the counter and plump down on banquettes along one wall to watch the corporate world conduct its business over lattes. If you're not up to eating much, you can always order their bread selection, which comes with award-winning Lot Eight dipping oil. If there's any sun you'll want to sit outside; on hot days the park fills up, so customers merge with the office workers getting stuck into their packed lunches. (04) 473 8500, www.astoria.co.nz

Next door to Astoria is classy interiors store *Cranfields*, opening onto Johnston St. Well worth a look for stylish homewares, sweet baby gifts and a very good selection of cards. (04) 499 4336, www.cranfields.com

Magnetix has moved from its spot next door to Astoria, around to 39 Johnston St, where Wholly Bagels used to be. They stock all the craft magazines you've ever dreamed of — if your passion is Oriental carpets they can sell you a mag to match, as long as you've got a spare $100. And they're open at 6.30am weekdays. (04) 472 2820, magnetix.co.nz. Around at 110 Featherston St, Tim and Glenda Skinner at *Capital Books* keep an extensive range of craft books, along with nautical and computer titles. (04) 473 9358, www.capitalbooks.co.nz

Even though they no longer have a fabric department, *Kirkcaldie & Stains*, Wellington's grand old department store across the block from Midland Park, is worth exploring. (04) 472 5899, www.kirkcaldies.co.nz

Up the little side street opposite the park is *Bears with Attitude*, Clare Cordery's tiny bear cave where creations such as Wellingtonian Jan Cuming's 'Elspeth' hide. Shop 3, 2 Woodward St, (04) 472 3277, www.bearswithattitude.co.nz

You could be excused for thinking there's not much room for craft in this very corporate city. But even in Parliament House, MPs have been known to knit their way through boring speeches. Parliament has some wonderful textile artworks that you can see as part of standard tours. The late Malcolm Harrison — named Creative New Zealand's inaugural Craft/Object Art Fellow in 2004 — designed *These are Matters of Pride* as a foil for the four-storey-high granite and stone Galleria. It's the largest public artwork commissioned in New Zealand, with panels inspired by our land, sky and seas, soaring above the Galleria, a light-filled central area that was closed in as part of a refurbishment of Parliament House. Down at ground level is the Mooring Stone, where ribbons placed by immigrant cultures are still being added to the work representing the ethnic groups that make up the fabric of New Zealand society.

Then there's the splendid wool and woven flax work *Whanaungatanga*, designed by Harrison, stitched by 700 embroiderers from groups around the country, and mounted on material woven by four Maori weavers. Based on stories from the Alexander Turnbull Library's Oral History Archive and Radio New Zealand 'Spectrum' documentaries, it hangs on Stair Seven — which unfortunately means it can't always be seen when Parliament is in progress. You can post cards from the foyer shop, so they're postmarked 'Parliament'. Guided tours leave from the foyer every hour; closed some public holidays — see their website for details: www.parliament.govt.nz, (04) 817 9999.

Up the road at *Wellington Cathedral*, Beverley Shore Bennett's pastel patchwork *Dossal Hanging* is a stunning backdrop on the wall behind the altar. The hanging can be seen through the glass front doors, but for a closer look the cathedral is open to the public weekdays 9am to 5pm, Saturdays 10am to 4pm and Sundays noon to 4pm — and of course you can see it from a distance during morning worship at 10am. (04) 472 0286, wellingtoncathedral.org.nz

If you're looking for crafty inspiration as well as gorgeous flowers Vanessa Prockter's *Woodstock* delivers. The textiles graduate also stocks handcrafted treats by Wellington designers, from Sue McMillan's Seam cushions (see Sue's (s)wheatheart project page 182) to goodies made from fabrics by such as Cath Kidston and Amy Butler. Diagonally across from Perrott's Corner, where she started out, at 134 Willis Street, (04) 385 2305. www.woodstockflorist.blogspot.com

Back down to town and if it's fabric you're after, good old *Arthur Toye* has moved down the road into the back of the Grand Arcade, (04) 473 6942. Where would home sewers be without this family business, now with five branches throughout the country? Be aware that traffic has been rerouted around here — watch out for buses and stick with the pedestrian lights.

Across the road you'll find fantastic craft and art books at the much-loved independent bookseller *Unity Books*, still going strong after 42 years and now in its fourth reinvention at 57 Willis St. The cards are legendary. And for those overcome by choice, there are armchairs at hand. (04) 499 4245, www.unitybooks.co.nz

Further up Willis St at no. 149 is *Quoil*, a contemporary jewellery gallery and workshop where rings, bracelets and brooches with textile content are sometimes on show. (04) 384 1499, www.quoil.co.nz

Vessel, around near the *Lido Café* in Victoria St, stocks the very best of New Zealand terracotta, stoneware and porcelain, by Katherine Smyth, Paul Melser and Raewynne Atkinson, among others, and also soft treasures — Jane Henry's elegant merino wraps plus lightly felted New Zealand wool blankets by Klippan of Sweden. Tea towels and cards include the Nice Work range

by Wellington book designer Sarah Maxey.
87 Victoria St, (04) 499 2321, www.vessel.co.nz

The most enduring legacy of artist Gordon Crook, who died in late August 2011 aged 90, is perhaps the appliquéd banners that hang in the Michael Fowler Centre. Part of the original decoration of what was intended as a 'new town hall', they hang in the Renouf Foyer on the first floor. The MFC is open from 8am to 5pm. The foyer is sometimes closed: telephone first if you want to see the banners. (04) 801 4231.

You'll recognise *Small Acorns'* new premises on the corner of Wakefield St and Blair, in the Courtenay quarter, by the patterned lemon exterior pillars. The first person in Australasia to have a Designers Guild concept store, Amanda Holland loves fabric and wallpaper and also stocks some divine baby gifts, including Maileg's Matchbox Mice. (04) 499 5795, www.smallacorns.co.nz

What is there to say about *Te Papa* that hasn't already been said? Of course, there is craft here, and fashion too, often in current exhibitions. Te Papa has regular back-of-house tours of collection stores, but to look at lace, costumes, and Maori and Pacific items in the collection you need to phone and make an appointment to see the appropriate collection manager. (04) 381 7000, tepapa.govt.nz. And Te Papa's Store brings together a representative range of New Zealand craft, cards, books, toys and garments. (04) 381 7013.

One of the best things to happen in recent years is the development of Wellington's waterfront. You can walk from Te Papa to the *New Zealand Academy of Fine Arts* on Queens Wharf, which often has exhibitions of embroidery, quilts and other fabric art — a banner out front advertises the current show; (04) 499 8807. Across the courtyard in the old Bond Store is the *Museum of Wellington City and Sea* (entry free), which gives a fascinating glimpse into early Wellington and the people who made it. (04) 4728 904, www.museumofwellington.co.nz

In a wee block of shops off Kent Terrace, Martha Craig has opened her second *Wanda Harland* shop, following the success of her Petone design store. 24 Elizabeth St, Mt Victoria, (04) 385 7778, www.wandaharland.co.nz

Cuba Quarter

Dealer galleries include *Peter McLeavey* at 147 Cuba St and *Bartley and Company Gallery*, 56A Ghuznee St. Tucked in between *Bowen Galleries* and *Hamish McKay* at 35 Ghuznee St is *Quilters Bookshop*, which shares a frontage with the small-but-perfectly-formed *Milk Crate* café. John Quilter's second-hand hardbacks are conventionally shelved; paperbacks pile up on a vast central table, inviting reckless purchasing, and he also buys and sells antique maps. (04) 472 2767.

Along on the corner of Marion St is Eleanor Steel's *ES Design*, which specialises in retro style using vintage fabrics. Her reputation for tackling difficult reupholstery jobs, either on the stash of old chairs in her warehouse or on those supplied by clients, is unsurpassed. She also does cushions, lampshades and whole interiors, and usually has a basket of fabric offcuts for fossickers. 1–5 Marion St, Te Aro, (04) 939 7899, www.esdesign.co.nz

Just up Marion St, longtime craft suppliers *Golding Handcrafts* was for sale as this book went to press and may finally have to close. They've served their customers well since 1979, stocking all sorts of things you couldn't find elsewhere. Thanks for everything, Goldings.

Nearby on the corner of Ghuznee and Taranaki sts are several floors of *Salvation Army* store, with some textile treasures to be found.

Before you set off back up Cuba St, nip down into Cuba Mall to the home of all small things quirky, *Iko Iko* at 118 Cuba, (04) 385 0977. Then head back up to pre-loved clothing treasure troves *Hunters and Collectors*, 219 Cuba St, and *Ziggurat Fashion Emporium*, 144 Cuba St.

Wander back up Cuba and its side streets just for the unrefined feel of the place — earthquake regulations may mean much of this will go forever, even before a big one. The further up you go, the cooler the cafés and more interesting the retail mix. Many emerging fashion stores specialise in recycled vintage fabric, and you can usually get a park right outside Wellington's *Global Fabrics* shop, in no-exit Garrett St; (04) 801 8887. There's a *Knit World* store, too, at 210B The Left Bank, inside Cuba Mall. (04) 385 1918.

For quality New Zealand souvenirs pop in to the *Save the Children* concept store, where they have everything from organic cotton kids' gear to scented candles and cards. 137 Cuba St, (04) 802 5149, www.savethechildren.org.nz

Theresa Gattung and Margaret Doucas's recycled designer chic shop *Eva's Attic* has a new premium store at street level at 174 Cuba St, selling top designer labels such as Trelise Cooper and Voon. It's open seven days, 11am to 5pm. Upstairs, the Attic sells discounted and non-designer bargains Thursday to Sunday. Set up two years ago in honour of Margaret's mum, the volunteer-run organisation has already raised over $40,000 for charity. (04) 381 3474, www.evasattic.co.nz

The Roman goddess of crafts — among many other things — gives her name to *Minerva*, the relocated textile bookshop and gallery, and offices of *New Zealand Quilter* magazine, in buzzing Upper Cuba St. Formerly resident at Taia Hall in Kilbirnie, the bookshop — which already stocked the largest number of books about textiles anywhere in the country — is now even bigger. The gallery is a more intimate space here, showcasing the best New Zealand fabric artists. The quarterly magazine, which covers a wide range of textile stories, is produced here, behind the shop. And there's a delectable range of wools and felt for crafters. 237 Cuba St, (04) 934 3424, www.nzquilter.com

Upper Cuba St is home territory for Victoria University's Faculty of Architecture and Design, so there are cheap ethnic eats everywhere, plus some cool cafés like *Olive* (sit out in the sunshine at the back), *Rick's Lounge* and the refurbished *Matterhorn*, which also has an outdoor eating area. Up past Minerva and across the motorway bypass, on Karo Drive, is the lovely *Martha's Pantry* tea shop. The original pantry was under the stairs in the draper's shop Mary McLeod bought two years ago for her calligraphy business; it's now part of a tea shop run by Mary's daughters Ondine and Anita McLeod. Mary says one old man burst into tears when he entered the light-filled premises, complete with drapery counter, creamy pink-and-white-and-green teapots, flowery china cups and saucers, embroidered tablecloths and fresh posies on each table. It reminded him of his mum, she says — and Mary and I have shared memories of our own mums over dainty servings of cupcakes and sandwiches. There's parking straight off the west-bound motorway bypass — or pull into the parking lane before Thistle Hall, on the corner of Cuba. 276 Cuba St, (04) 385 7228.

Back down on Ghuznee is *Satay Village*, a favourite cheap-and-cheerful restaurant, where the owner remembers regulars' orders, no matter how long since they were last in. 58 Ghuznee St, (04) 801 8538.

If you're looking for books at bargain prices check out *Arty Bee's Books* at their mega-store down at The Oaks on Manners St, for the desirable, the rare and the bizarre, as well as a constant turnover of crime and kids' books. They'll buy your surplus volumes too. (04) 384 5339, www.artybees.co.nz

Along at 90 Dixon St is *D. Alexander Interiors*, where colour-coordinated bolts of cloth, and hanging racks of samples from every designer from Antarctic to Zoffany provide inspiration. They keep a selection of one-off cushions made up from remnants of the latest luscious fabrics — and for those in search of a bargain, there's always a bin of discarded swatches and longer end lengths, just the thing for a new Roman blind or your own homemade cushions. (04) 385 0360, www.dalexandertextiles.co.nz

Rag-trade veteran Chrissie Potter's bright orange *Fabrics Direct* offers tempting yardage to home sewers whether for furnishings or fashion, at 97 Ghuznee St, near Willis, with parking outside. (04) 385 6767.

Before you leave this side of town, pop up to the *Nairn St Colonial Cottage* — Nairn St is just off the top of Willis St. The cottage has been declared of 'outstanding significance' by the Historic Places Trust — and it's a real thrill to visit this 1858 survivor. You can see quilts that came out with the original European settlers plus rag rugs, a beaded lambrequin embroidered by one of the daughters of the house, and other textiles that softened the harsh life of the pioneers. Curator Kim Townley will bring out books of wallpaper samples from Victorian times and dress your preteen up in a shoulder corset as part of the museum's education programme. Summer hours are 10am to 4pm daily; winter hours are noon to 4pm weekends and public holidays. (04) 384 9122, www.colonialcottagemuseum.co.nz

Out on its own in Karori is Suzy Miller's *Piece by Piece*, a charming little quilt shop just off the main road in Marsden Village. Everything is neatly organised here, including cheerful Souleiado fabrics from Provence — those classic hard-wearing cloths the French called 'indiennes', which make great napkins and tablecloths as well as country-style quilts. Irresistible! Shop 3, Marsden Village, 149 Karori Rd. A No. 3 Karori Park bus will drop you virtually at the door. Closed Sundays. (04) 476 0480.

Kilbirnie via Newtown

Out at Newtown there's a cluster of antique shops on Riddiford St near the lights at the intersection with Adelaide Rd, before you get to the hospital. Then in the shopping centre is design store *Juniper*, at 14 Rintoul St, (04) 389 4058, and on

Constable St, which links the heart of town to the seaside suburbs and airport over the hill, is darned good fair-trade coffee at *People's Coffee*.

Up the road is a cluster of shops including Andrew Missen's *Nidus*, at 74 Constable St, with an intriguing assortment of New Zealand-made recycled and reassembled furniture, art and some stunning ceramics. Open Fridays and Saturdays, 10am to 5.30pm. (04) 380 1632.

Jeanie McCafferty's *Next Stop Earth*, sells the freshest flowers from Thursday through Saturday, plus all sorts of goodies from cards to soap and lashings of lollipop-coloured recycled plastic containers from Spain. For kids, there's a tempting array of things most gardeners would rather not know about — mock bugs, butterflies and other critters. (04) 389 0408.

At 91 Constable St, furniture designer-maker *Duncan Sargent* works from home and doesn't mind people popping in. 021 138 8482, www.duncansargent.com

Kilbirnie has changed. Where Taia Textile Gallery and *New Zealand Quilter* magazine were there's now an animal charity op shop. Around the corner is *Kim's Curios*, tucked into an elderly shop on the corner of Rongotai Rd, under the hill. Veteran antique dealer Kim Skinner followed her heart to the capital after years of commuting from Milford in Auckland. As well as elegant china she has jewellery, sterling silver and special baby collectables from nursery china and Fun-Ho toys to vintage and classic baby clothes — newly knitted by Kim herself. Closed Sundays and Mondays. 2 Rongotai Rd, Kilbirnie, (04) 387 2808, 021 539 237.

Around the corner is John and Ruth McIntyre's *Children's Bookshop*, where many a successful New Zealand children's title has been launched. Known to 'Nine to Noon' listeners for his passionate fortnightly radio round-ups of the best books for children, John stocks over 10,000 titles, presided over by uber-knowledgeable staff. Closed Sundays and public holidays. Shop 26, Kilbirnie Plaza, (04) 387 3905, www.childrensbookshop.co.nz

Wellington Sewing Services has grown from a fantastic repair service to a shop offering everything for the quilter and knitter, plus long-arm quilting machines. Shop 3, Kilbirnie Plaza, 22 Bay Rd, (04) 387 4505.

Paul Rivers' *Asia Gallery* has been a source of much joy to my fabric-loving friends, and not just because of the vintage kimonos and other fabric he stocks, augmented weekly from his warehouse and replenished quarterly from Japan. We've found all sorts of small treasures — boxes, chests and so on — plus lacquerware and jewellery, much of it antique. 5/23 Bay Rd, Kilbirnie, (04) 387 3488.

They don't come much craftier than the folk at Weta Workshop. The *Weta Cave* at Miramar is a mini-museum that gives the public an insight into the award-winning creative processes that feature in movies such as *The Hobbit* and *The Adventures of Tintin*. Cnr Camperdown Rd & Weka St, (04) 380 9361, www.wetanz.com

While you're in Miramar, stop for a coffee or lunch at *The Larder*, or check out the elegantly reinvented *Roxy* cinema and café in the shopping centre at 5 Park Rd, Miramar, (04) 388 5555, www.roxycinema.co.nz

But if you've only time to visit one café this side of the capital, and you fancy a Cook Strait view, try the rebuilt *Maranui Surf Life Saving Club*. It's my favourite place to hang out before catching a flight from nearby Wellington airport — but choose your time if you don't want to be cut off at the ankles by racing toddlers. The coffee is good, the muesli magnificent, and they do a tasty line of wholesome salads at very good prices; the green tea noodles are most satisfying. A window seat offers stunning views over Lyall Bay, a favourite windsurfing spot. 7 Lyall Bay Parade, (04) 387 4539, www.maranui.co.nz

For quick tasty takeaways, the dishy little sister café *Queen Sally's Diamond Deli* offers similar food and coffee. Worth a visit for the decor, a down-home blend of repurposed Greek olive cans, original painted sarking and vintage grocery signs. 200 Queen's Drive,(04) 387 2829.

Thorndon Tripping

Across in Thorndon, the *Katherine Mansfield Birthplace*, not far up from the bottom of Tinakori Rd at no. 25, is also a beauty. Even the garden is planted in authentic style. Allow a good hour if you can: there are some textile treats in this 1888 townhouse, and a very good little gift shop. Parking can be difficult here — pull into the driveway if you're stuck. Open daily except Christmas Day and Good Friday. (04) 473 7268, www.katherinemansfield.com

Even without Nancys Embroidery (now on Thorndon Quay), Tinakori Rd has much to offer. There are antique shops, interiors stores and gift shops, a couple of pre-loved designer-label clothing stores, and *Flowers Rediscovered*, the sort of florist's shop that makes you want to step in and simply breathe deeply. (04) 471 1021.

Just up from the Bowen St lights, on the corner of St Mary St is Stephanie Bruce's *Wall St*, worth a look for its wallpaper and interior treats. Check out Florence Broadhurst classics and New Zealander Ben Masters' quirky botanical designs. 352 Tinakori Rd, 04 499 8684, wallstdesigns.co. nz. Next door at no. 356 is *Memory Lane Antiques*. (04) 499 2666.

Sadly, retro-rich store *Strangely Familiar* on the other corner has gone — but owner Katrina Dormer still offers splendid tea parties in your own home and has an online shop. (04) 476 2218, www.strangelyfamiliar.co.nz

Down a back alley behind the lights at 344 Tinakori Rd is Mary Clare Wilson's enduring *Cherry Orchard Antiques*, where you might find French torchons and quilts for sale among the stock she brings back each year from trips to Europe. (04) 499 8533.

Millwood Gallery at 291B Tinakori Rd offers a great selection of children's books, art books, quilt calendars and artworks. (04) 473 5178. Next door, *Tinakori Antiques* repays a close look, especially in their out-the-back building, housing less expensive china and other goodies. (04) 472 7043.

Think French country with a dash of English manor house . . . Bernice Ryan's *Vintage Antiques* mixes armoires, antiquarian books, elegant

antique mirrors and old — sometimes monogrammed — linens. With a background in the rag trade and a past as a quilter, Bernice can't resist samplers and French linens. She replenishes her stock annually on visits to Europe, seeking out everything from dress forms to garden sieves. You can also stay in her B&B, *The Bay Window*, just down the road (see page 122). 318 Tinakori Rd, (04) 473 3250, www.vintageantiques.co.nz

The post-industrial mix of zinc, retro chairs and French urban antique that is *Zinc+* is the child of Trish Jenkins and her husband Dave. A snappy combination of zinc-topped dining tables, new French ticking on old deck-chairs, and refurbished filing cabinets meets the French bric-a-brac known as *brocante*. Best buy? Uber-cool perforated steel lightshades with red cross diffusers, in sizes to order. Open seven days. 320B Tinakori Rd, (04) 891 0281, www.zincplus.co.nz

A tantalising mix of old, new, borrowed — but never blue — fills *Unearthed*, snuggled into a black weatherboard building that's been recycled many times. Everything from kitchenalia to silk souvenir scarves is crammed into Christine McDonnell's wee shop — 'quirky, ethnic, retro and down-to-earth'. Look for seventies glass, sixties tinware and a warm welcoming dollop of red, orange and yellow ceramics and plastic on a central table. Open Wednesday and Thursday 11am to 4pm, Friday and Saturday 11am to 5pm, 302 Tinakori Rd, 021 036 9439.

Opposite Unearthed, Antiques dealer Elizabeth Wilkins is back from the beach (well, Paraparaumu, anyway) and installed in Nancy's old shop. (04) 892 0059, while up the road, Val Whisker of *Bush Telegraph* has come to town with country-style furniture.

Down on Thorndon Quay, once the city's waterfront, is *Nancys Embroidery*, formerly of Tinakori Rd. Colourful, creative and always bustling, Nancys — one of the oldest-surviving craft enterprises in the country, set up in 1967 by the late Nancy Robb as an embroidery bar in the James Smith department store — has moved into larger premises with plenty of parking outside. Over the years, hooked rugs have given way to patchwork, embroidery and knitting — but you still get expert advice from friendly staff. And there's always someone stitching in the classroom at the back: students in one of their many classes, or owner Mary Self, designing another pattern or kit for her label Stitchnz. Open seven days. 241 Thorndon Quay, (04) 473 4047, www.nancys.co.nz

Across the road is *Bordeaux Bakery*, one of the first French cafés in the capital, while further along, tucked away in the heart of Thorndon's Woolstore complex, is *Le Marché Français*. It's a celebration of all things French, with a café offering authentic bistro food plus a deli with fabulous sheep's, goat's and cow's cheeses to try, and French treats including the legendary biscuits Rose de Reims by Fossier, long the traditional dipping sweet for Moët & Chandon's Rosé bubbles. Worth it for the hot pink tins alone! 262 Thorndon Quay, (04) 494 1834, www.lemarche.co.nz

One of the more recent craft revivals is catered for by *Craft House*, who have everything for scrapbooking in their new store around the corner at 47 Hutt Rd. It's fun for kids too. (04) 499 4499, www.crafthouse.co.nz

Along at Kaiwharawhara is another Gallic treat, François Febvre's *La Cloche* bistro, next to Shelly BMW. François cooks up vast quantities of brown onion soup — the real thing, made from scratch

— as well as omelettes and sweet treats such as tarte au citron. And, of course, café au lait made the French way. 134 Hutt Rd, (04) 473 4892.

Nearby, opposite the Ngaio Gorge lights, there's *Spotlight*, with a large parking lot out the front; (04) 472 5600. Next door is the relocated *Fabric Warehouse*, in the building that used to house a pot warehouse. Growing up in the rag trade, boss Stephen Shaw probably cut his teeth on a pair of pinking shears — he's kept his hand in with this ever-popular Aladdin's cave of fab fabrics from the latest dress materials to odd lines he's found on back shelves, stuff like old Viyellas and interesting furnishing yardage. He doesn't sell patterns but keeps catalogues for reference; weird and wonderful notions and braids pop up too. His generosity to the capital's fashion and textile students is legendary. 126 Hutt Rd, (04) 473 8150.

Perfectly Petone

You really need wheels to get to Lower Hutt, but Petone is easily reached by train or bus as well as by car. Although it's only 10 minutes from the capital, Petone is a world away in attitude. The revitalised main street, Jackson St — just a block from the beach and parallel to the waterfront — has become a mecca for collectors, with a string of design and homeware stores, fashion boutiques, gift shops, second-hand dealers and recycled-clothing shops, plus some very good coffee outlets.

Knitters will be delighted to find Tash Barneveld and her team at *Holland Road Yarn Company* knitting up a storm in a small, rainbow-hued store, conveniently opposite St Vinnie's. Tash has impeccable heritage: her grandmother Margaret Stove, author of a new book on knitted lace, is the doyenne of New Zealand knitters; Tash herself has designed and knitted everything from fancy sock patterns to guerilla knitted seats for the local bus stop. She stocks hand-dyed Knitsch sock yarn and merino lace yarns, all hand-dyed in Wellington, and has even persuaded Stansborough (see page 142) to spin a knitting yarn from their heritage Gotland sheep. 281 Jackson Street, (04) 891 0760, www.hollandroadyarn.co.nz

Urban Mythology at 155B Jackson St is the only New Zealand source of some stunning furnishing fabrics from Turkey: limited amounts of embroidered cottons, hand chosen from the mill, with offcuts from curtaining and cushion orders there for the picking in a big bin. Owner Sandy Palmer has now also acquired D. Alexander Interiors in town (see page 130). (04) 939 3369, www.dalexandertextiles.co.nz

For op shoppers there are plenty of outlets here, including *St Vincent de Paul, Te Omanga Hospice and Salvation Army* stores.

Village Beads at 129 Jackson St has a full schedule of classes for adults and children, including during school holidays; (04) 566 3240. Petone also has a thriving scrapbook supply shop, *Scrapbook Central*, out at Unit 8, Bouverie St, around from Mitre 10 Mega. (04) 939 5127, www.scrapbookcentral.co.nz

The effervescent Gloria, formerly of Trentham Treasures, opened her Petone retro store *Petone Treasures* on the day of a major storm — but that didn't stop a swag of well-priced furniture pieces and china walking out the door. Housed in her uncle George Wing's verandahed former green-grocery store, Gloria's combined store has me popping in weekly to keep an eye on treasures. 186 Jackson St, (04) 568 5805.

One consequence of the making of *The Lord of the Rings* and *The Lion, The Witch and The Wardrobe* has been the revival of old crafts, including handweaving. Petone firm *Stansborough* made cloaks for the movies from their grey handspun, heritage-breed Gotland wool and now produce fine designer textiles for sale to the public. 'A Window into the Past' gives visitors an idea of the way it was when the 1890s Victorian weaving looms were operating. 22 Sydney St; open Tuesdays and Thursdays from 9.30am to 2.30pm. (04) 566 5591, www.stansborough.co.nz

My favourite coffee stop in Petone is the very low-key *Go-Bang Espresso*, with coffee to match its name — they roast their own (Ripe) and you can sit outside. There's also *Villi*, *Figg*, *Flax*, *Palace* and *Lemon Squeeze*, all within a couple of blocks.

Up on the Western Hutt hills lives the elegant *Ruth Meier*, who may well have New Zealand's largest collection of buttons — she once bought a truckload, in Zurich. Ruth is happy to share her knowledge and show her collection by appointment, (04) 586 2692. She also makes handsome button necklaces which she sells at Minerva's Christmas show each year.

Eastbourne Escape

You won't find craft supplies in this seaside village around the far side of Wellington Harbour but there's plenty to inspire crafty girls in the little shopping centre. If you come by ferry from Queens Wharf in town, you'll find the village a short walk from Days Bay Wharf. Days Bay itself has one of Wellington's oldest craft outlets in *Van Helden's*, which still sells lots of ceramics and silk scarves. (04) 562 8191.

The bays and the flat area known as Muritai — the setting for Katherine Mansfield's story 'At the Bay' — each have their own character, but the best way of starting to explore Eastbourne proper is in Rimu St. There you can still buy meat from the butcher, fresh fruit and veges from the greengrocer, groceries from Four Square, and freshly churned ice cream from Gelissimo. There's also a good deli, several cafés and restaurants, the library and a computer shop.

Then there are the shops loaded with ideas for crafty girls. *Kevin and Ruby* takes its name from owner Deby Smith's cat and artist Annie Haywards' dog; the stock includes embellished felt cushions and lampshades, delicate, whimsical jewellery made from glass and china fragments, and Jason Kelly's send-up signs. (04) 562 7838.

Across the road on Rimu St is *Montage*, (04) 562 7188, which also stocks a range of work from Kiwi crafters, while *G&L Antiques*, around on Muritai Rd, deals in period furniture with a good line in decorative accessories like chandeliers. (04) 562 8705, www.glantiques.com

Rona Gallery and Bookshop has moved to larger premises on Muritai Rd, and still sells great books as well as featuring artists such as Darcy Nicholas and Wellesley Binding.

If you've had enough crafty stimulation you can walk on the beach: take a stroll in Days Bay or park your car at the end of the road for a full-on four-hour walk to the historic Pencarrow lighthouse, the first in the country to have a female keeper.

When you need somewhere to lay your head, Eastbourne has some good B&Bs. Bet and Wal Louden's *The Anchorage* is within a block of the village at 107 Marine Parade, (04) 562 8310, while *The Walnut Tree* also comes highly recommended; 335 Muritai Rd, (04) 562 8768, thewalnuttree.co.nz

The Hutt Valley

Five minutes' drive north of Petone is Lower Hutt's CBD, and the city's undoubted star, *The Dowse*. Plan on taking a lunch break here in their pleasant café *Reka*, with its outdoor seating and the best coffee north of Petone. There's plenty of pay-and-display parking. *The Dowse* specialises in applied art, and their exhibitions often include textile works. The collection includes quilts by textile artist Malcolm Harrison and The Family, a collection of 30 dressed cloth dolls that have toured the country and make an appearance from time to time. (04) 570 6500, www.dowse.org.nz

Evans's, at 224 High St, is one of two surviving stores in the Evans family's once extensive chain. Thirty years ago, it was easily the best place to buy winceyette for your winter pyjamas, plissé for summer shorties, and your baby's nappy fabric by the metre. Now you can get a good range of supplies for cross-stitch and tapestry, teddy bears, patchwork and quilting — plus bridal and evening wear. Open seven days. (04) 569 2075.

Langi's Island Styles, which also used to have a Porirua branch, moved to Lower Hutt as the gentrification of Petone has meant their customers have moved north up the valley. They still have plenty of Pacific print cottons. My most exciting discovery at Langi's was a handstitched tivaevae, one of a chestful of quilts created in the 1960s in the Cook Islands. They're now in the collection of *New Zealand Quilter*. 233 High St, (04) 568 2807.

A tiny antique and collectables shop in High St, in a block of shops where the street turns into a residential zone, is well worth a visit. *Three Buckets Full* has been a well-kept secret for more than 15 years, but if you yearn for buttons, lace and other tiny treasures you'll find something in Wendy Frith's carefully ordered sewing machine drawers and boxes. Just the thing if you're making clothes for antique dolls — which she also deals in. One wall is covered in strings of bright shiny beads, and there are always enticing treats on the $1 trolley outside (which is what first caught my eye). Wendy's good about holding items if you can't get there during opening hours: 11am to 5pm Tuesday to Friday, 11am to 2pm Saturday. 509 High St, 027 464 8800.

Upper Hutt is around 15 minutes away from Lower Hutt. For quilters and embroiderers, *Thimbles and Threads* is a destination in itself. Sharon Van der Gulik, one of the quilting industry's longest-serving members, opened her large shop in an industrial area behind the railway line at the top of Park St 20 years ago. There's a machine-quilting service available and she has added some stunning yarns to her vast range of fabric, threads, books and magazines. There's also a stock of pretty porcelain, soaps, candles and other gift lines. 40 Park St, (04) 526 6513, thimblesandthreads@xtra.co.nz

Upper Hutt has a splendid cultural centre, *Expressions*, that often features exhibitions of textiles. There's a theatre, two galleries, a gift shop and *Limelight*, on Fergusson Drive between the city council offices and the swimming pool. Open Tuesday to Sunday and all public holidays except Christmas Day. (04) 527 2168, www.expressions.org.nz

Cross the river at Silverstream bridge for Heretaunga St, the scenic route to Upper Hutt city through established trees and gardens. In Heretaunga, miniaturist Donna Leddy stocks everything for inch-to-the-foot dolls' house aficionados in her garden studio at 7 York Ave, a cul-de-sac off the main street. You'll find her at home on Saturdays between 10am and 2pm, creating her own miniature worlds as well as looking after the needs of local crafters. (04) 970 4025, www.hathawayminiatures.co.nz

Further north, at Te Marua, is *Stonestead Devonshire Teas* and *Sawmill Quiltery*. Kevin Bold's scones and cream are worth the trip out from town, even if you're not a patchworker looking to add to your stash — or coming to see quilts

displayed al fresco on Waitangi Day. If it's a hot summer's day, towering trees offer blissful shade, and it's a treat to wander around the old garden while the scones are cooking — choose from half a dozen teas and several home-made jams — and admire pear trees that might be older than the relocated house, built in 1860 and restored on site. Yvonne Matthews' quilt shop and Kevin's tea shop are open year round, Thursday to Sunday, from 10am to 4.30pm at 3 Plateau Rd, Te Marua, Upper Hutt. Sawmill Quiltery (04) 526 2517, www.sawmillersquiltery.wordpress.com; Stonestead Devonshire Teas (04) 526 6838.

Porirua, the Kapiti Coast and Points North

While Highway 2 follows the Hutt Valley north, Highway 1 goes up the Kapiti Coast. The first stop off the motorway is Porirua, worth visiting for *Pataka*, the museum of arts and cultures in Norrie St. It's part of a larger complex that includes the city library and a performing arts space. Pataka — which shows quilts and other textiles from time to time — also has a good café, *Kaizen*, and shop. (04) 237 1511, www.pataka.org.nz

Porirua is also a mecca for op shopping, and North City Mega Centre has a *Spotlight* store, (04) 238 4055. Sadly, Langi's Island Styles has gone (but they're still in Lower Hutt). There's also a *Knit World* with helpful staff at 62 Queens Dr, (04) 566 4689.

Further north at 99 Mana Esplanade, on Highway 1, is the *Short Poppy*, source of many treasures from Victoriana through to the seventies: old gowns, books, jewellery, tools, china and memorabilia — and the rest! (04) 233 2201.

Nearby, Billee Mutton, of *Unwind*, is at home at 25 Bodmin Tce, Camborne — basically during school hours on weekdays, or by arrangement, (04) 233 2045. She stocks supplies for needle felters, wet felters, spinners and weavers and will do repairs and take classes too. Billee bought Sheena Taylor's Ashford business when Sheena moved up to Waikanae; you can still buy from Sheena's *Socks 'n' Wool* business but her homestay has closed. 2 Te Maku Grove, Waikanae, (04) 904 1022, www.sheenas.co.nz

The short detour down to the beachfront road at Paekakariki is well worth it for *The Beach Store*, wallpaper designer Bridey Farrell and woodworker John Girdlestone's splendid collection of international and New Zealand labels from Tom Kluyskens' stools to Danish felted slippers and John's Crash Craft skateboards. Oh, and you can buy Supreme coffee and Rush Munro or Kapiti ice creams to take across the road to the very edge of the ocean. Open Thursday, Friday and Saturday 9am to 5pm, Sunday 10am to 5pm. 104 The Parade, (04) 292 8330, thebeachstore.wordpress.com

At Pukerua Bay, the last settlement before you hit the coast road proper, *Kathy McLauchlan* sells hand-dyed silk fibres and embroidery threads and knitting kits — think tea cosies, hand warmers and scarves — from her home at 2 Puketai Pl. Please ring first, (04) 239 9851, mclpad@xtra.co.nz

At Raumati Beach shops you'll find *Kapiti Coast Bernina*, with a good range of sewing and knitting supplies, a growing range of fabrics, plus great buttons, books and sewing machines. 4A Margaret Rd, (04) 299 1904, www.kapitibernina.co.nz

Fibre Flair at Waikanae has supplies for everyone creating textiles, from quilters, embroiderers, spinners and weavers to lacemakers, beaders and dyers. They also sell Pfaff sewing machines. On the main road at Waikanae just by the traffic lights, they're open six days a week from 9am to 5pm. (04) 902 9908, www.fibreflair.com

On a weekend or public holiday it's worth the detour to Waikanae Beach for Sue Wilkie's *Ma-Mite* at 32 Tutere St. Kiwiana spills out onto the footpath from a dark brown double hut that was once part of a camping ground, just down the road from the famous Front Room café. Sue's a fan of the great Kiwi bach and tries to stock everything from 'old dunger' surfboards and water skis — snapped up for decoration — and 1960s sun loungers, deck chairs and duffle bags to Formica tables, Crown Lynn cups, candlewick bedspreads to travelbags, tea cosies and pinnies. Ring out of hours and she may be able to open up for you. (04) 293 4074.

At Te Horo, en route to the outlet stores on Otaki's main street, is catering queen Ruth Pretty's home base, signposted on the main road. Just over the railway line, up a pretty drive is Springfield, where Ruth's team prepares for everything from weddings to VIP events. You can enjoy coffee and cake in the *Kitchen Shop* while browsing for gadgets, cookbooks, serving dishes and the prettiest linen teatowels ever. Open almost every day — check the website. 41 School Rd, (06) 364 3161, www.ruthpretty.co.nz

I've tried two B&B options at Te Horo, equally special in their own ways. *Te Horo Bach* is Arthur and Adrienne Kebbel's contemporary beach house at 44 Rodney St, at the untouched, wind-blown Te Horo Beach. The house was designed by their architect son Sam Kebbell; www.tehorobach.co.nz. The other is Susi and Vaughn White's *Lavender Creek Farm*, where separate Tuscan-style accommodation is surrounded by vineyards, a small olive grove and fields of lavender. 123 Settlement Rd, Te Horo, (06) 364 3682, www.lavendercreek.co.nz

Otaki's *Brown Sugar Café* is a sister to the Taihape one, with the same good coffee, melt-in-your-mouth Danish pastries made on site, and the prettiest garden setting. It's on the corner just north of the bridge as you come into town from the south. Plenty of room for children to run around, and some delightful cards and gift lines too. They're open from 9am daily. There's off-street parking on the side street if the kerbside is full.

On the way north into Levin, you can't miss Trish Tilbury's *Krazy Cow* quilting and craft, in the old Railway Station on Oxford St, the main street, emblazoned with a black and white and orange logo. Unfortunately the shop — like many such places — was closed on the Monday when I went through. Pity — it was raining cats and dogs, though not cows, and I loved the idea of an espresso or hot chocolate from their café. I'll definitely stop next time, and make sure it's not a Monday. Trish sells Pfaff and Janome sewing machines as well as the usual fabric, books, magazines, threads and a vast range of haberdashery. (06) 368 5077, www.krazycow.co.nz

Knit World in Levin is at 197 Oxford St, (06) 367 9700. The town is also a good place to trawl op shops — there's a large *Sallies* on the corner of Oxford St — and antique shops: on the opposite corner is *Levin Antiques*. Closed Sundays and Tuesdays. (06) 367 3699.

Further up the main street, Lynette Collis has taken the stock of *Cherry Pie Quilt Patch* into her Bernina sewing centre at 204 Oxford St, (06) 368 3680, cherrypiequiltpatch.co.nz. Cheryl Chambers, who started the business, now offers crafters' retreats at the former home of Cherry Pie Quilt Patch at 288 Arapaepae Road South, otherwise known as Highway 57 — the back road from Wellington to Palmerston North via Shannon. (06) 367 5220.

Shannon has becomea destination town, thanks to the efforts of artist Suzie Johnson. Among the boutiques are Glenn Harrison's *Generate*, formerly Box of Birds — I bought a supersized tea towel, complete with a classic Kiwi ice-cream slice, that will make a great party apron. 12 Balance St (Highway 57), (-9) 362 7711.

Antique dealer Jenny Dick has lots of textiles — scarves, embroidered linen, lace and a flurry of old fox furs — in her old bank building on the main road through town. *Legacy Antiques and Collectibles* is open every day from 10am till 5pm — or even later if you happen to just make it and want to browse. Plimmer Tce (the main road), (06) 362 7117, or email legacy_antiques@xtra.co.nz

And on the staircase going up is Elza Dissanayake's *Flowers on Lotus Lane*, mixing artificial with real to provide colour and perfume. Plimmer Tce (also Highway 57), 021 312 304.

A Weekend Away — the Wairarapa

Weary Wellingtonians like to head over the hill to unwind in the Wairarapa's small towns and the plentiful weekend cottages that are available for hire, often coming complete with a basket of goodies for leisurely brunches. Greytown, Carterton, Martinborough and Featherston are all less than 10 minutes' drive from each other and the region's big town, Masterton, is at the northern end of the string.

You can go upmarket and stay in themed rooms at *The White Swan Hotel* at 109 Main St, Greytown — (06) 304 8894, www.thewhiteswan.co.nz — or choose from a selection of bed-and-breakfast accommodation on www.wairarapanz.com

Martinborough bustles at the weekends, with cafés, restaurants, wineries and an ever-increasing number of fashionable shops all vying for visitors' dollars. You might like to plan to be in the town for the twice-annual Martinborough Fair — the first Saturday in February and again in March, when many local crafters sell their wares.

Featherston, the first stop over the hill, is coming alive. There's the incomparable Campbell Moon's long-established *Marsden Antiques*, within sight of the main street at 76 Fox St, (06) 308 9724. Along the road, in a light-filled little shop, is *Craft Country*, where local women Natalie Friend, Michele Stokes and Emma McCleary have collected work by 16 crafters from Hawke's Bay to Wellington — and they run their business strictly on a no-commission basis out of a shared love of craft. Open Thursday to Sunday 10am to 3pm, 44A Fitzherbert St, opposite the Post Office. www.craftcountry.wordpress.com

Once you reach Martinborough there are several incentives for crafty girls to get out and shop. Angela Sears recently refurbished her *Heritage Shop* at 33 Jellicoe St, the oldest of the town's vintage shops. She's been there 12 years, but only embroiderers and keen collectors seem to have found her — perhaps because Jellicoe is the street running from the Square down to Lake Ferry, and isn't on the café run. Angela buys her stock at auctions and picks up all sorts of new, old and certainly a lot of unfinished textiles — tablecloths, tapestries, edgings, laces, buttons, work baskets. She has some craft and spinning supplies (looms, wheels, wool) at her next-door shop, *Waihenga Trading Centre* and furniture as well. Open Friday to Monday, 10am to 4pm. (06) 306 8495.

Meanwhile, round on Kansas St, just off the Square, in a house built for the town's postmaster back in the 1930s, is Daphne Geisler. She paid tribute to her mother-in-law when naming her shop *Gertrude Snyder Vintage Treasure*, though these days it's easier to find it as Vintage Treasure. Daphne had always dreamed of being a second-hand dealer — as a child in the UK she would go with her granny round church fairs collecting tins of buttons. She likes the fact that she can fill each room of her ex-state house with appropriate gems — cooking implements and everyday Crown Lynn in the kitchen, vintage clothes in the wardrobe. And she has never subscribed to the dealers' mantra that you shouldn't have likes and dislikes — 'I sell what I like to live with every day,' she says. 021 611 035, www.vintagetreasurenz.com

Mixing old kitchen goodies with new is part of the style at *Mint*, just off the main street at 14D Ohio St, where tried and true items such as time-worn scales and transferware are slipped into fresh new designer ranges. (06) 306 6240, www.mintatmartinborough.blogspot.com

We stayed in the delightful *General Store* holiday cottage, set among olive groves, yet close enough to walk to the village. Once a general store in Eastbourne, on the edge of Wellington Harbour, the cottage has a huge claw-footed bath and offers fabulous breakfast provisions with luscious local produce — not surprising since owners Jan and Roger Barrett once had the deli in the seaside settlement and now run a catering company. 027 249 8024, www.providorefood.co.nz

Before you leave Martinborough, call into *Thrive*, set up by sisters Josie and Sophie Bidwill in the main street just as the town was taking off. As well as their own label Thrive, they stock Kate Sylvester, Standard Issue, Birkenstock and Hema Oils. And, of course, Thunderwear. You'd be surprised just who wears proudly New Zealand-made Thunderpants (sorry, my lips are sealed) which come in a range of wild colours sporting designs by Sophie. Best of all, they're made only in organic cotton, with a wee bit of Lycra for fit. 8 Kitchener St, (06) 306 8991, www.thunderwear.co.nz

If you have the time it's worth heading north via the back roads to Greytown, a picturesque settlement that was the first place in New Zealand to celebrate Arbor Day — several gum trees in the main street were the first exotic trees to be planted in the country.

As you come into Greytown from Martinborough you'll see the sign for *Kane Carding*, wool classers Denise and Guy Sandall's business supplying sliver for felters and merino for spinners, among other things. Visitors are welcome but it pays to ring first. 149 Bidwells Cutting Rd, (06) 304 9470, www.kanecarding.co.nz

Back on the main street in Greytown, *Schoc* is housed in a 1920s-era confectionery store in the Cobblestones Early Settlers Museum at 177 Main St. Sample before you buy their divine chocolate, 'crafted to be eaten not stored', according to the tobacco-pouch-style label on blocks of rose geranium, tangerine, white chocolate with cardamom and dark with chilli. The small studio also shapes handmade chocolates in French moulds, and at Christmas they offer frankincense-and-myrrh-flavoured chocolate, rubbed with gold leaf. (06) 304 8960, www.schoc.co.nz

Open since 1999, *Crafters Heaven*, next door at 169 Main St, stocks a wide range of supplies for embroiderers, quilters and crafters. They're the Wairarapa dealers for Brother sewing machines and Ashford wheels and they do mail order. (06) 304 8477, www.craftersheaven.co.nz

Across the road at 206-208 Main Street is Viv and Rosy Wilson's *Chestnut Gallery*, specialising in dolls' houses and furniture. (06) 304 7005, www.chestnutgallery.co.nz

On the right as you come in is J.O.Y., James Herbison's petite shop celebrating the Joy of Yarn, behind Scarlet Oak Cottage at 143 Main St. A sock knitter, James was among the first to import special sock yarns, which incorporate some nylon to reinforce toes and heels — but since others starting bringing it in he's begun dyeing his own Fibre Alive range of fingering — what we know as 4-ply — used in sock knitting. James has a day job ('born to knit, forced to work') so if you want to visit outside of the regular Sunday Knit-Teas and Friday Sock Clubs, please ring first. (06) 304 9805, www.joyofyarn.co.nz

A little further on, in the shopping centre, stop for pizza or coffee at the award-winning bright pink *Cuckoo* café, 128 Main St, (06) 304 8992, or *The French Baker* further up the street (on the right) for coffee and a slice of their superb chocolate tart or brown sugary cinnamon rolls. Their hazelnut muesli is darned good too. 81 Main St, (06) 304 8873.

Greytown is full of treasures, from small galleries to antique shops and newer gift shops. My favourites include *Kouka*, in a heritage cottage southside of the *White Swan Hotel*, where Nigel Thorp sells old books and some textile treasures including, on the day I visited, a 1930s felt tea cosy. Closed Tuesdays and Wednesdays. 027 244 2991.

At *Hope and Glory*, formerly of Martinborough, is Vanya Wilkinson who worked for some time for Colefax and Fowler in the UK. She sells 'Found,

Made and Cherished' objects, many of them textile and many sourced locally — 'all the things I love, so nothing's left out'. She shares a space with Sam Beesley's *The Tool Box* (also in Petone) which specialises in blokey and industrial stuff like the incredible army medic's wicker hamper and a couple of canvas cases used to carry NZBC outside-broadcast gear last century. (06) 304 8834, www.hopeglorynz.com

Next door to The French Baker, in the historic Lemon Tree Cottage, is the small but beautiful *Moonflower* florist, where Rebecca Dagarin, daughter of florist Jill and antique dealer Campbell Moon, sells wee textile treasures made from vintage cloth as well as exquisite flower arrangements. (06) 304 8925, www.moonflower.co.nz

Emporos, at 75 Main Street, has ends of gorgeous furnishing fabrics as well as antiques. (06) 304 8603.

Design guru *Michael Nalder* — he who styled the White Swan, among other things — now has a purpose-built showroom bringing together his interior design practice and retail business: trademark antiques, jewellery, glass and rare treasures from his regular jaunts to Bali, all against a backdrop of gorgeous handprinted Fornasetti papers by Cole and Sons. Closed Tuesdays. 65 Main St, www.michaelnalder.co.nz

Carterton, a bustling country town, is home to several good antique and second-hand shops but you just have to take a chance on these, since their opening hours are erratic.

Fuzzy, which specialises in retro, is open Saturday, Sunday and Monday only. (06) 379 5650.

Just around in Park Rd is crafter Leanne Taylor, who trades under the name *Ramari Textiles*. She's got the cutest little shop, which was once an army hut, where she sells all sorts of soft stuff — tea cosies, bags, cushions, lovely linen overall pinnies, badges and other things made from felt souvenir pennants. 80 Park Rd, (06) 379 9163, www.ramaritextiles.blogspot.com

The town has a large paua factory that does a roaring trade with tourists. Paua has lost some of its kitsch rep — if you're wanting to play with the stuff, you could have a look at the paua shell factory shop at *Paua World* for pretty buttons that are also sold in places like Te Papa's store. (06) 379 4247, www.pauashell.co.nz

Kaye Keene, of 91 Lincoln Rd, Carterton, still makes around 500 Rich Little Rag Dolls a year. You can visit her at her home studio where she makes practical dolls and dolls' clothes that can stand a bit of washing. She also shares her own collection of dolls with visitors. (06) 379 5583, www.ragdolls.craftplaza.co.nz

It's worth stopping at Masterton for several reasons. *The Embroidery Shop* at 250 Queen St stocks all sorts of goodies for knitters and embroiderers. They've been very involved in a Hats for Heads project at the local hospital, crafting beanies for newborns, and they'll even knit up your wool for you if you can't deal with it! (06) 377 1418.

Quilters will love *Quilters Lane*, in the lane behind the library on Queen St, the main street. Sheila Boakes' shop has a huge range of 100% cotton and linen fabrics as well as accessories and tools, threads and embellishments, and she also offers classes and the chance to pin your quilts out in a generous workshop space. Open Tuesday to Saturday. 50A Queen St, www.quilterslane.co.nz

Then there's *Aratoi*, Wairarapa's Museum of Art and History, on Bruce St, which opened in February 2002. Its gift shop sells textiles such as mohair rugs, and the exhibitions are worth following, since embroidery is sometimes on the menu. *Café Entice* serves Supreme coffee. Closed only on Christmas Day and Good Friday, (06) 370 0001, www.aratoi.org.nz

Masterton also has a good independent bookseller in *Hedley's Bookshop*. 150 Queen St, (06) 378 2875.

If you can't resist cheek-caressing fluffy stuff you'll be as delighted as I was to find *Masterweave Textiles'* factory shop at 39 Lincoln Rd, in the heart of town. Lindsay and Philippa Cairns started their business 10 years ago while still goat farmers; that's made way for making luxurious textiles from mohair fibre. They also weave blankets, throws, rugs and scarves from alpaca and wool, and sometimes have leftovers from overseas orders in unusual colourways. If you're passing through out of normal office hours, Lindsay will arrange a time to meet you at the factory. (06) 378 8891, www.masterweavetextiles.com

If you're needing a cuppa or want to see some of New Zealand's rare bird life, stop at *Pukaha Mt Bruce National Wildlife Sanctuary* for refreshments while looking out the window at takahe. The latest arrival is Manukura, the first white kiwi born in captivity. www.mtbruce.org.nz

In Pahiatua you'll find *The Crafty Pear* patchwork shop (06) 376 8842, and several good op shops — *The Op Shop*, on the right going north, and the much bigger *Sallies* across the road.

If you keep on driving you'll reach Woodville, which is covered in the Taranaki/Manawatu chapter.

Wallpaper Fantail Decorations

1. Trace off, and cut out, the fantail stencil opposite page, marking the six points at the base of the tail.
2. Cut a piece of wallpaper* twice as big as the fantail (180 x 120 mm) and fold in half, wrong sides together.
3. Place the fantail stencil on the wallpaper and trace around it, with a fine, but visible, pen or pencil (this will be chopped off).
4. With a pin, prick holes through the base tail points into the wallpaper.
5. With coloured / matching thread, start at the top, leaving threads long to become part of the hanging loop.
6. Stitch down to each pin hole at the tail base, and up again, 3–4 mm in from the drawn line.
7. When back to the beginning, back stitch over the starting point and leave threads long to create a loop.
8. Knot threads together at the ends, leaving 100–150 mm for the hanging loop; trim threads past the knot.
9. Cut around the fantail, just inside the drawn stencil line, being careful not to trim off the loop threads.

* Any stiff medium-heavy paper can be used, such as wrapping paper, old calendar images, postcards, drawer-liners, vinyl/duraseal, packaging, etc.

DESIGNED BY: GENEVIEVE PACKER, WELLINGTON

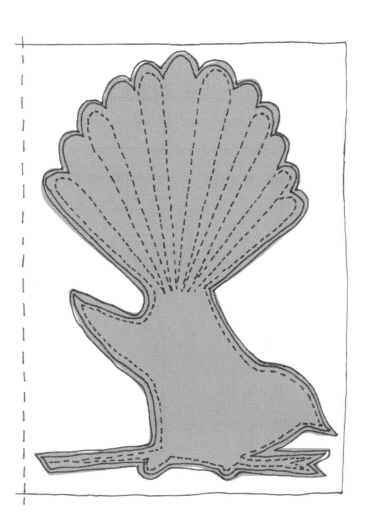

Chapter Seven

THE TOP OF
THE SOUTH ISLAND

N° 11

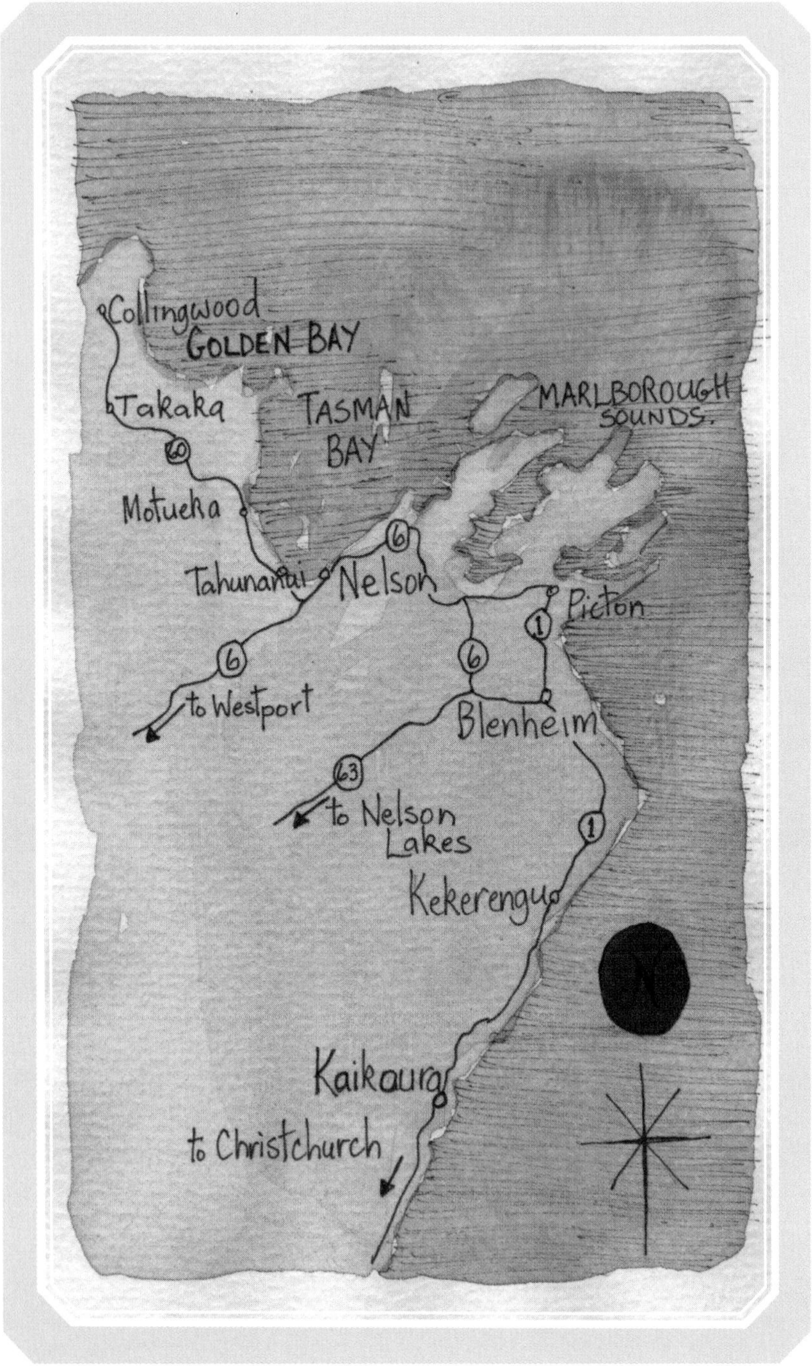

Collingwood
GOLDEN BAY
Takaka
60
TASMAN BAY
MARLBOROUGH SOUNDS.
Motueka
6
Tahunanui
Nelson
Picton
1
6
6
to Westport
Blenheim
63
to Nelson Lakes
1
Kekerengu
N
Kaikoura
to Christchurch

Picton is the gateway to the South Island for many people, giving access to Marlborough — and on to Christchurch — or to Nelson, Golden Bay and then the West Coast.

While the Bluebridge and Interislander ferries may no longer be the cheapest way of crossing Cook Strait — budget airline fares have snatched that record — the boats certainly move more travellers than anyone else. Even if your crossing has been less than perfect, you can sit back and relax once inside the sheltered waters of Tory Channel.

If you've brought your own car, you can simply drive off onto Highway 1 on arrival. There are also rental car offices right at the ferry terminal, or you can catch a shuttle bus to Christchurch or the TranzCoastal train, which stops at Blenheim and Kaikoura en route.

Picton has reinvented itself in the last decade, losing some heritage buildings but acquiring a more integrated foreshore and a landscaped waterfront that presents a pretty picture to the arriving world. The marina at nearby Waikawa Bay is the second largest in the country after Auckland, and you can get a water taxi from the wharf at Picton to outlying bays and coves.

For food, before heading out of Picton, pull off the road on the corner of Auckland and Dublin Sts for some excellent Dutch baking from the long-established *Picton Village Bakkerij*.

Then if you're going to Nelson, you have a choice of route. The picturesque Queen Charlotte Dr winds its way around the shore of Grove Arm before reaching Havelock, New Zealand's mussel capital, where it meets the main road. At Havelock, stone carver and sculptor *Clem Mellish* is at home at 4 Wilson St by appointment; (03) 574 2472. After that there are several hilly stretches before you reach the glistening shore of Tasman Bay for the run into Nelson city.

The alternative is to go south to access the Nelson road through grape country, turning right at the little town of Renwick. Pelorus Bridge, where the road takes a kink across a narrow bridge, is a nice place to stop for a cuppa — you'll be needing one by then.

Wine Country

Renwick is also the junction with Highway 63, the route through to the West Coast via Nelson Lakes. We had a pleasant night at a vineyard a few kilometres out of town, as a guest of B&B hosts and winegrowers Nettie Barrow and Jane Craighead, who along with Nettie's husband Bill built the *Straw Lodge* complex a decade ago. The latest accommodation is a standalone cottage surrounded by lavender. They've a shed full of bikes ready for you to ride the surrounding stopbanks or long straight roads. 17 Fareham Lane, RD1, (03) 572 9767, www.strawlodge.co.nz

In Renwick itself is the tiniest, most chock-full wool shop I've ever squeezed myself into. Margaret Gage is a legend in the trade and can find anything in the apparent chaos of her wee shop, *Renwick Nic-Nacs* at 16 Uxbridge St, which doubles as the town's information centre. Look for the sign that says 'Booking Agents'. I bought some circular needles I'd been meaning to find, and a pair of All Black booties for our new grandson Jack, a Sydneysider. While I was there at least six other people came into the shop for some wool or haberdashery requirements. (03) 572 9615.

Nearby there's a tiny local museum, the kind you can just walk into at any time to marvel over relics of a bygone era through glass windows. It's not frozen in time though — when I visited they were about to get a new exhibit featuring the history of that New Zealand institution, the *School Journal*. *Renwick Museum and Watson Memorial Library*, next to Post shop, High St.

At home, by appointment, in the Boyce St studio and home she designed herself is textile artist *Catherine Lawes*, who moved back to New Zealand in 2008 after a long period in the UK. She makes quilts, bags, wall hangings and what she calls 'one-off extraordinary garments' using saris, silks and velvets. She also sells hand-dyed fabric and experimental packs. (03) 572 8325, www.catherinelawes.com

Rapaura Rd is one of a grid of long straight roads that runs between Blenheim and Renwick. Crafty girls and their blokes will definitely want to call in to *The Vines Village*, 10 minutes from Blenheim or less from Renwick, opposite Grosvenor Estate winery. *The Quilter's Barn*, the patchwork business now owned by Anne Murchison, has moved to the back of the purpose-built barn, behind Swazi.

Anne has a separate wool shop two doors along. You can also taste wine and liqueurs, sample olives and oil, sit yourself down with a coffee overlooking an artificial lake or just lick a Kapiti ice cream or sample the sweetness at *Fudge House* — run by Anne's sister Heather — we loved the lemon meringue and nougat varieties. Open seven days 10am to 4.30pm. Off-road parking. (03) 572 7240, www.thequiltersbarn.co.nz

For a vineyard lunch nearby, try Allan Scott Winery's *Twelve Trees* on Jackson's Rd, a courtyard restaurant offering sheltered al fresco dining as well as tables indoors to soak up the sun when the wind blows. (03) 572 7123.

One other stop I loved was *Makana Confectionery*'s boutique chocolate factory, on the corner of Rapaura and O'Dwyers Rds. It's like something out of *Charlie and the Chocolate Factory* — visitors are offered a beautifully presented sample of the day to try, and you can watch chocolates being made through a viewing window. There's another factory in Kerikeri. 0800 MAKANA (0800 625 262), www.makana.co.nz

Back in Blenheim, the *Millennium Art Gallery* on Seymour St is always worth a visit — we were lucky that we were there in time for an exhibition of regional artists' work as part of the Real New Zealand Festival.

Richmond, Nelson, institution *Soucheby's Antiques* have recently opened a shop in Blenheim, at 50 Grove Rd on Highway 1, (03) 579 6046.

South to Kaikoura

From Blenheim we headed south on Highway 1, not stopping until we reached *The Store* at Kekerengu. Taking a break here has become a ritual for a lot of travellers en route to Kaikoura. Roughly halfway between Blenheim and the Kaikoura Peninsula, this knob sticking out on the coast was just a place to stop for petrol 10 years ago. Now it's a sprawling café that offers everything from good coffee and casual snacks to local delicacies like crayfish. And the setting is sublime, with plenty of possies on the deck, looking out over grassy lawn to the stony beach and rolling waves. Make the most of it and stretch your legs; you may come across a wedding party from nearby St Oswald's Church. In winter there are log fires in big open hearths. Open seven days. Parking straight off the road. (03) 575 8600, www.the-store.co.nz

Pull off the road at *Ohau Point* for a special wildlife treat. Hide all your belongings away and lock the car, then cross the main highway with caution and follow the bushy track beneath the rail bridge. A five-minute walk leads to a pool below a waterfall where young seal pups endlessly practise their rolls and twirls, to the delight of all those prepared to step out of their cars.

At Kaikoura, best known these days for its whale watching, *A Patch of Country* has changed owners and moved across the main road to the seaward side — all of which has improved the experience for passing quilters. New owner Rachel Baxter has a large range of fabric, craft supplies, gifts, classes and Janome sewing machines — plus local alpaca yarn for those who like souvenirs to take back home. 22 Beach Rd, (03) 319 5465, www.apatchofcountry.co.nz

And conveniently outside there's a coffee cart selling Atomic Fair Trade coffee. *The Coffee Hit*, (03) 319 5144.

For tourists, Kaikoura has a branch of the well-known *Woolshed Galleries* which also can be found in Hanmer Springs and Akaroa. Check out their daily specials in sheepskin, merino and possum/merino. 10 Beach Rd (the main road), just before the Whale Watch turnoff, (03) 319 7979, www.woolshednz.co.nz

Fyffe House is Kaikoura's Historic Places Trust treasure. Perched on whale vertebrae at the far eastern end of the town beach on Fyffe Quay, this 1860 pink-washed cottage with its dormer windows offers a fascinating insight into the life of whaling pioneers. Closed Tuesdays and Wednesdays in winter. (03) 319 5835.

The local *Kaikoura Museum*, just off the main road at 14 Ludstone Rd, is worth a look too, with some textile treasures you can ask to see. These include an 1880 counterpane of embroidered flowers on a black wool suiting background and a delightful pair of naive embroideries stitched in the early 1920s on huckaback. One depicts 'A Dance at Hapuku Hall in aid of the Piano Fund May 19th 1922', and from 1917 there's a skilled interpretation of the colours of the Nelson Infantry Regiment, worked by a recuperating Anzac soldier in an English hospital. (03) 319 5831, kk.museum@xtra.co.nz

Accommodation offerings here include a very smart backpackers' hostel, *Albatross Backpackers Inn*, at 1 Torquay St. (03) 319 6090, www.albatross-kaikoura.co.nz

Nelson to Golden Bay

Wearable Art is what springs to mind these days when Nelson is mentioned, although with the show's move to Wellington in 2005 much has changed. But Nelson — stretching to include Golden Bay — is hugely well organised when it comes to craft in the broadest sense. This dates back to the earliest days of the Nelson Provincial Arts Council, which set out to market the region's then-hidden craftspeople. These days the comprehensive regional guidebook *Art in its Own Place* has become a model for other regions. Now into its sixth edition, it lists heritage homestays and flash lodges as well as food, wine and (of course) artisan enterprises. The $15 publication also offers a critical overview of various disciplines, plus some fascinating historical background on this earliest of New Zealand European settlements. Many Nelson craftspeople can be visited in their studios by appointment. This means planning your itinerary ahead if you want to meet special basketmakers, weavers and feltmakers, rather than simply trusting that you can view their work in galleries. Others are happy to be dropped in on — during opening hours of course — notably those in collective arrangements out in the country, like the *Grape Escape* complex at Richmond. If you're really keen to cover the field, buy the guidebook. www.nelsonartsguide.co.nz

The *Saturday Market* has long been an institution in Nelson. Held in a city carpark, it's a mecca for artists and their customers, as well as the perfect opportunity to stock up with bread, cheese, salami, nuts, preserves, fresh fruit and veggies (often organic) and maybe a second-hand book to take to your homestay accommodation. There's plenty of soap, candles and other crafty products too. Open 8am to 1pm. There's also a smaller Sunday fossickers' market from 9am to 1pm.

 If you miss the markets, there are heaps of other options. Head for the beginning of Waimea Rd, where *Jimpy's Antiques* has been satisfying treasure-seekers for many years. I didn't go away empty this trip either — I snaffled a couple of pieces of nursery china for the grandkids and a selection of cross-stitch panels for my daughter Genevieve, who recycles them into cushions, bags and even lampshades. There I met Sue Wootton, from the Ferry Antique Centre in Christchurch, for the first time. She also collects textiles and was buying some to take home.

Next door, Paul at *Toy Toy* loves his toys so much most are not for sale — but you can put down a gold coin and visit his wee museum specialising in toys from the sixties, seventies and eighties. Open Tuesday to Saturday at 4 Waimea Rd.

 A few blocks away, just behind the cathedral on the corner of Tula and Nile Sts, is *Tula and Niles*, (03) 545 6959, in a refurbished villa with some delicious tropical palms and bamboo furniture plus great art-deco clothes and collectables.

 Christine Ross and Barb Christian's *Vintage* has become well-established at 50 Vanguard St. They're especially strong on kitchenalia, but there are also reupholstered sixties chrome chairs and couches, a big rack of vintage clothing, lots of china — plus LPs for those vinyl collectors travelling with crafty girls. Open Monday to Saturday 11am to 5pm, near the roundabout; parking at the rear, off the street. (03) 548 7060, vintage-shop@hotmail.com

Eclectic, another former Waimea Rd tenant, now occupies two storeys in Hardy St with one of the most comprehensive collections around. A trip to the US last year netted vintage fabrics the like of which I've not seen — huge sprays of violets on chintz covers are one of the latest fabric finds — and there's a whole room full of textiles. This is surely the only antiques website that literally sparkles on screen — a reflection of the larger-than-life Maria Henare rather than her quieter husband Shane. 254 Hardy St, (03) 548 3940, www.eclecticantiquecentre.co.nz

The Suter Te Aratoi o Whakatu, Nelson's public art gallery at 208 Bridge St, has the cream of local craft artists' work in its shop, including woven wearable moths by Deborah Walsh and crocheted metal flowers by Andrea Chandler. The Suter also has a great café — good food and a pleasant view out to Queens Park. Open 10.30am to 4.30pm daily except Christmas Day. (03) 548 4699, www.thesuter.org.nz

If you didn't stop at the Suter, you'll be desperate for a coffee by now. One of my favourite places is Kay Field's *Morrison St Café*, in a historic building at 244 Hardy St. Sunny spaces spill out onto al fresco areas, there's local art for sale on the walls, and local mags and info to pick up and read. (03) 548 8110, www.morrisonstreetcafe.co.nz

Nelson has some long-established craft outlets right in its very walkable town centre, of which the *Fibre Spectrum* cooperative is perhaps the best known. In their historic building at 280 Trafalgar St, near the cathedral, they offer a big selection of spun, woven, knitted and stitched garments, decorative accessories and yarns for you to play with. Exhibitions change monthly. (03) 548 1939, www.fibrespectrum.co.nz

Also on the main street, several blocks down, *Page & Blackmore* is a splendid independent bookseller, where you can buy a copy of *Art in its Own Place* as well as books about local artists, craftspeople and history — and the latest newspapers and magazines. 254 Trafalgar St, (03) 548 9992, www.pageandblackmore.co.nz

Nelson's 'oldests' include the oldest museum in the country, the *Nelson Provincial Museum*, now housed in a very accessible building on the corner of Trafalgar and Hardy Sts, a block down from the cathedral. Check out the latest exhibitions, and browse and possibly order from the extensive photographic archives, including the Tyree collection. (03) 547 9740, www.nelsonmuseum.co.nz

In the same block on Hardy are three crafty places in a row. *Cruella's* is the sort of wool shop you won't walk out of without some new yarn and needles — manager Jessica is an American whose enthusiasm for knitting is contagious. Here's a cave glowing with colour not only from shelves filled with yarn — spun from the alpacas, yaks and coloured sheep grown by owner Ruth Benge and her husband on their Golden Bay farm — but also from garments knitted up from their Rare Yarns range, which includes the most gorgeous textures, in exclusive patterns. If you're in town on a Tuesday evening or Wednesday morning, come along to Stitch 'n' Bitch sessions to meet other knitters and share your creative challenges over a cuppa. Closed Sundays. 155 Hardy St, (03) 548 4016, www.cruellas.co.nz

Either side of Cruella's is the incredible *Bead Gallery*, another visual treat, whether you're a maker or not. Laurie and Barbara Johnson were some of the earliest folk in the country to fall

under the spell of beads. Formerly housed in a renovated cottage in a light industrial area, their Aladdin's cave of glittering, glowing and eminently stringable beads has moved into two shops in town — one stocking everything you'll need to make your own beads, the other for those who just want the finished product, often one-off samples. They also have stores at Richmond and Picton. Open seven days at 153 Hardy St, (03) 546 7807, www.beads.co.nz

Along the road at 118 Hardy St, *Creations Unlimited* sewing and craft centre has everything you could want for patchwork, embroidery, rugmaking, paper crafts and bears. Their knitting wools include possum and merino mix, the shop sells four different sewing machine brands and they have drop-in classes too. (03) 548 4297, www.creationsunlimited.co.nz

For bargain-priced fabric try *Morelands* at 34 Vanguard St, (03) 548 8875.

The *Swedish Bakery & Café* at 54 Bridge St is my newest Nelson find. 'Swiwi' (Swedish/Kiwi) couple Dennis and Bronwyn Eriksson and their Swedish baker make traditional treats such as pepparkaka and biskvi, plus artisan sourdough breads — the bread menu changes daily. They also import elegant textiles, which have been woven for over 300 years by the Swedish family Ekelund. Closed Sundays. (03) 546 8685, www.theswedishbakery.co.nz

Next to them is Margaret and Dave Prebble's *Bernina* shop, (03) 548 4882, while across the road at 53A is Jo Menary's *Shine*, a funky design store with just the sort of gifts you might treat yourself to, including jewellery. (03) 548 4848.

Along at the western end of Bridge St is *Red Gallery*, still great advocates for local artists and designers under new owners Sarah Sharp and Caroline Marshall. The superb little café offers a select but tasty menu and their cards are worth checking out too. 1 Bridge St, (03) 548 2170, www.redartgallery.com

 If you fancy sitting outside on the banks of the Maitai River, which runs from the hills down into the harbour, try *Oasis* café and bar, (03) 548 1180. It's right next to the Information Centre by the bridge on Trafalgar St, at Millers Acre, where Nelson began. It's just a short walk along the riverbank to Peter Elsbury and Zoe Buchanan's contemporary jewellery workshop and gallery *Lustre*, at 36 Collingwood St, which also sells some textile works. (03) 545 8922, www.elsbury.net

 Nelson's well off for op shops — the *Sallies* are on the edge of the Montgomery Square carpark, while the enlarged *Hospice shop* is on Bridge St. I found a Liberty blouse at the tiny *Lifeline* shop in Collingwood St and another at the *Red Cross* shop at Tahunanui on the way in from the airport, where the office person was kind enough to reopen for me. 59 Parkers Rd, (03) 546 4570.

While you're in the area, seize the moment and walk on the magnificent sands of Tahunanui Beach: just park the car and step onto flat sand that's endless and reviving.

Ten minutes from town — and just two from the airport — the WOW complex is the home of the *World of Wearable Art & Collectable Cars*. Past Wearable Art winners parade endlessly, lit by the special effects that make the annual show so spectacular. There's a great café here, and a good range of crafts. The cars, polished to perfection, are as scintillating as the wearable art. Open seven days from 10am. Closes 5pm in winter, 6.30pm in summer. (03) 548 9299, www.wowcars.co.nz

At Richmond, 13 km south of Nelson or Highway 6, is *Richmond Antiques & Curios*, one of my favourite antique shops — and another source on this trip of 'tapestries' for my crafty daughter. It's up the hill a little, above the town centre, on the corner of Queen and Salisbury Sts, with a back entry that's full of the kind of old stuff film companies use for props. Closed Sundays. (03) 544 7675.

Also at Richmond, at 75 Gladstone Rd, the main road going south, is *Soucheby's Antiques*, (03) 544 0723. It was pouring with rain when I called in but they didn't seem to mind — the shop was full of dripping customers. They don't have much in the way of textiles but it's still worth a stop — even in the rain — for vintage toys, old musical instruments and other unusual objects. Soucheby's Petone shop has now closed, but they have recently opened one in Blenheim. www.antiquesnewzealand.co.nz

Out on its own at 40 McShane Rd is *Eyebright*, a country store with just about everything in a purpose-built barn with a beautiful garden next to it, established in 1986 by Adrienne and Peter Owen. Jewellery, kitchenwares, silk flowers like you've never seen and Christmas decorations all year round. (03) 544 4977, www.eyebright.co.nz

At Brightwater, Mary and Selwyn Hall have their *Hallblacks* 'woollery', selling everything for spinners, weavers, felters and knitters. They have toilet facilities, coffee and tea, and are open all hours, but advise phoning first. 57 Mt Heskington Rd, RD1, (03) 542 3411, www.hallblacks.co.nz

We took ourselves off for a quiet weekend in the country at *Wisteria Cottage*, a wee place behind the Wakefield home of former Wellingtonians Annie Fraser and Liam Gallacher and their daughter Paige. Out of an old cottage on the property they bought a former schoolmaster's house — lawyer turned interior decorator Annie has created the perfect country retreat, set in pretty gardens under deciduous trees. It was a wet weekend when we were there, but we just stoked up the woodburner and hunkered down on the comfy couches with our knitting and books, enjoying the solitude. 271 Wakefield-Kohatu Highway, (03) 541 9590, www.wisteriacottage.co.nz

Craft Habitat at Richmond has gone, as has quilt shop My Back Porch, at Bronte. But new at Tasman, just back on the old main road from the Motueka end of the Ruby Bay bypass, is *Jointworks*, the combined studio of weaver Jane and woodworker Tony Clark. They're installed in the old general store at 413 Aporo Rd, in Tasman village. Jane is the daughter of Christchurch weaver Anne Field, who lost her Arts Centre studio in the quake; Jane retrieved some of her own scarves, wraps and knee rugs from the ruins. Tony and Jane are in their studios most days from 9.30am to 5pm, other times by arrangement; they also go to the Nelson market. (03) 526 6171, www.jointworks.co.nz

Not far from Jointworks is ceramicist *Steve Fullmer*'s gallery at 3 Baldwin Rd, (03) 526 6765. At the other end of the bypass, at 56 Mapua Dr, former Wellingtonians *Ann and Bob Phillips* have their woodturning studio. (03) 540 2467, www.rubycoastmouterehills.co.nz

Down at Mapua Wharf, the *Cool Store Gallery* has a very cool range of classy work from over a hundred Nelson and West Coast artists. Closed Mondays in summer, Tuesdays as well in winter. (03) 540 3778, www.coolstoregallery.co.nz

Mapua Country Trading Co. has practical stuff for your garden and home, with an emphasis on sustainability. (03) 540 2246, www.mapuacountrytrading.co.nz

Delicious, at Coolstores 4 & 5, has more interiors and homeware goodies, with a spectacular theatrical setting for their kids' books and toys. Open 11am to 4.30pm Wednesday to Sunday. (03) 540 2463.

Right on the water's edge looking over the estuary, *The Apple Shed Café and Bar* serves breakfast and lunch every day from 9am and dinner Tuesday to Sunday from 5pm. (03) 540 3381, www.appleshed.co.nz

Kim Lineham is a passionate dolls' house maker and miniaturist whose home studio at 80 Gardner Valley Rd in Upper Moutere is open by arrangement. (03) 543 2576, www.kimsminis.com

Motueka is a busy town servicing the needs of orchards, a growing number of vineyards and visitors to nearby Kaiteriteri Beach and Abel Tasman National Park. It has some good cafés — try Maggie Le Long's *Red Beret*, at 145 High St. Sadly, it no longer has the excellent gift shop behind. The *Patisserie Royale* has delectable baking, and there's a good Indian restaurant — *Simply Indian* — in the middle of town.

Needleworx Sewing & Needle Crafts is right on the main street too, with dressmaking and patchwork fabrics, wool, haberdashery and patterns. 168 High St, (03) 528 4528, www.needleworx.co.nz

One of my favourite places, a short drive over the hill from Motueka, is Abel Tasman National Park — and I'm fortunate to be able to visit more often than most because my sister and brother-in-law own a lodge at Marahau, gateway to the park. I've done a fair bit of writing at *Abel Tasman Marahau Lodge* over the years, and some time each day there's the chance to walk in the park itself — either alone or in the company of my sister — to Stu's Lookout, where you survey Tasman Bay from a high peak. What a gift. (03) 527 8250, www.abeltasmanmarahaulodge.co.nz

It's an hour over the hill to Golden Bay from Riwaka — though you may wish to drive in first to the awesome source of the Riwaka River. At the top of Marble Mountain you can visit Ngarau Caves, where the water drips down through rock layers to arrive at that source.

Textile artist Morag Dean is one of the artists who sells at *Monza Art Gallery* in Takaka. Philly Hall's had her vibrant shop filled with local artists' work for over a decade now — there's everything from painting to stunning flax weaving. Sarah Hornibrooke uses natural plant material such as reeds and flax to make her stylised birds, weaves harakeke into kete, and twists wire to shape a menagerie of horses, pigs and other animals. Open 10am to 5pm in summer. 25 Commercial St, (03) 525 8510, www.monza.co.nz

Nestled in a bush garden overlooking the Parapara estuary, 22 km from Takaka, is Rosie Little and Bruce Hamlin's *Estuary Arts*. Look for their handsome rusted cutout sign on the roadside and drive in to a haven of natural plantings around the studio they built in 1987. Stunning art, from ceramics, glass and decorative tiles to paintings, is inspired by the landscape around them. They're closed in winter, open October to mid-April, Wednesday to Sunday, 9am to 5pm, and Monday and Tuesday at holiday periods. Maybe ring first to be sure they're open. (03) 524 8466, www.estuaryarts.co.nz

Living Light Candles may be sold throughout the country but it's nice to be able to turn down a little country lane in Takaka and see — and smell — freshly made examples. While the factory itself is not open to visitors, the Living Light Gallery at Tukurua Rd has a full range of stock and specials to choose from. One of their four designers, Ngaire, sells work under the name Stitchbird on crafty website felt.co.nz. Opening hours vary depending on the season — ring first. (03) 525 7575, www.livinglightcandles.co.nz

Vera and Reto Balzer's *Sans Souci Inn* at Richmond Rd, Pohara, on the eastern side of the endless Golden Bay beach, has stood the test of time. Handbuilt from adobe, the 'inn' is a collection of spacious private rooms with comfortable beds (plus an ecological toilet system and communal washroom). At the inn you can have slow-cooked evening meals as well as sumptuous breakfasts — or you can prepare your own.
(03) 525 8663, www.sanssouciinn.co.nz

You may find the tiny museum along the main street of Takaka open — or the tides could be right for a trip to the lighthouse at Farewell Spit. *Farewell Spit Eco Tours* have been taking visitors out for over 60 years, originally in old Bedford Trucks. These days a more sustainable form of transport is called for — but it's still a fitting way to end your Golden Bay trip. 0800 808 257, www.farewellspit.com

Wheat Bag

CALICO INNER

1. Cut a large, stretched-out palm-sized heart shape for the template on card or paper.
2. Draw round the heart onto 2 thicknesses of calico fabric.
3. Cut out the heart shape and machine stitch the calico pieces together using a small stitch, leaving a small opening for filling the bag.
4. Three-quarters fill the bag with clean whole wheat (suitable for wheat bags).
5. Hand stitch or machine stitch over the opening. Note: The inner calico bag doesn't need to be turned inside out as it sits inside the wool blanket bag.

WOOL BLANKET OUTER

1. Draw a round heart shape onto 2 thicknesses of washed wool blanket.
2. Cut out the heart shape and machine stitch the pieces together using a small stitch, leaving a large opening on one of the straight sides to insert the calico inner.
3. Turn the wool heart inside out so the raw edges are inside the bag, and insert the calico inner.
4. Turn the straight raw edges into the wool bag and blind stitch along the opening.

TO FINISH

Appliqué your choice of felt trim — a cross or flower — or an old blanket label that doesn't have any metallic thread.

TO USE

Microwave on high for 3 mins on a clean plate with a half glass of water on the side — relax and enjoy!

DESIGNED BY: SUE MCMILLAN OF SEAM.CO.NZ

Chapter Eight

THE WEST COAST

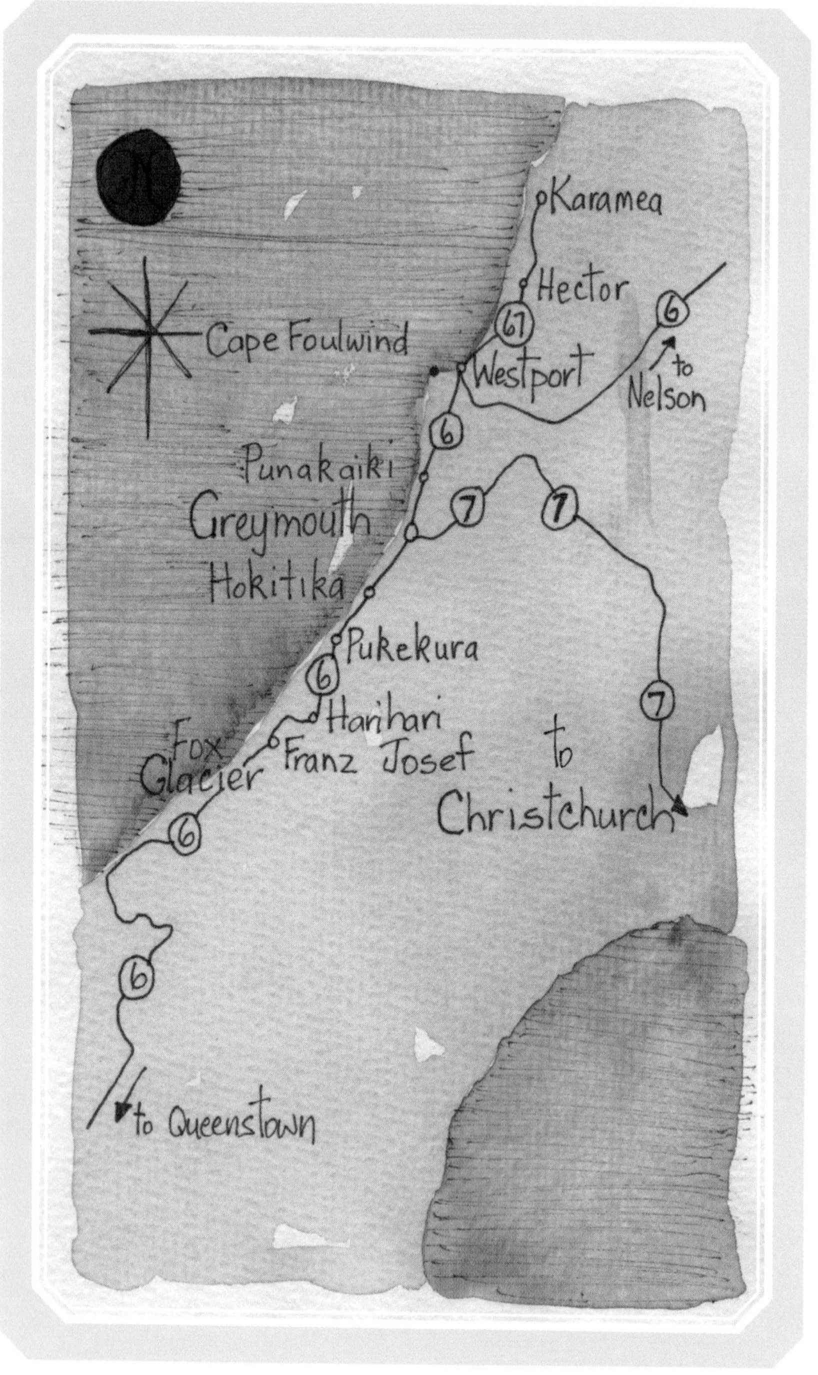

Karamea
Hector
67
6
Cape Foulwind
Westport
to
Nelson
6
Punakaiki
Greymouth
7
7
Hokitika
Pukekura
6
7
Harihari
Fox
Glacier
Franz Josef
to
Christchurch
6
6
to Queenstown

Most visitors hit the West Coast at Greymouth, whether by car, plane or train, so that's where we'll start. If you arrive for the day on the splendid TranzAlpine train service from Christchurch, you'll have an hour before you have to return to the east coast — time enough to explore the town.

Better by far, though, is to book a night at a local bed-and-breakfast and go back the next day, as I did the first time I visited. I've included a trio of accommodation options between Westport and Karamea, and there are several more good ones out at Cape Foulwind.

Get your first coffee at the laidback *DP1 Art Café* in Greymouth, looking across at the river stopbank. (03) 768 4005.

The *Bernina Shop* in 40 Albert St, in the main shopping area, has good craft supplies and general sewing needs as well as dress fabrics. (03) 768 4463.

There are at least five good op shops in the vicinity, including one across the river at cold-as-charity coaltown Cobden.

Well-known local quilter Barbara McQuarrie often exhibits — sometimes in association with her potter husband Bob and textile-artist daughter Caroline — at the *Left Bank Art Gallery* on the corner of Tainui St, on the left bank of the Grey River, looking out to sea. It's well worth a visit to see its greenstone taonga, as well as local artists' work. Open seven days, (03) 768 0038, www.leftbankarts.org.nz

Between Greymouth and the smaller town of Westport, going north, is Punakaiki — a bustling stop in the middle of nowhere, with good craft for sale and an award-winning café offering prices to suit all pockets in a spectacular setting. Do the walk around the famous Pancake Rocks — the path is wheelchair-friendly and doesn't take long.

The much-lauded Bay House restaurant — a café by day, restaurant by night and a gallery for local art all the time — has relocated from its stunning setting on the Cape Foulwind coastal route into Westport and been reinvented as *The Town House*. It's near the port end of Westport, on the corner of Cobden and Palmerston Sts, and includes a cosy bar. They suggest you reserve a table. (03) 789 7133, www.thetownhouse.co.nz

Keep going north if you have the time; Karamea, tucked away at the top of the West Coast, is best known for its spectacular, end-of-the-world scenery, and is well worth a trip.

In Westport itself ceramicists John and Anne Crawford have their *Hector Gallery* at 116 Palmerston St, (03) 789 6378, or you can call at their studio on the road north to Karamea, on the coast at Ngakawau, (03) 782 8107. Choose a classy souvenir, inspired by the local beach, to take home with you — I'm still thrilled with my pale celadon bowl with its gently pointed sides. They also offer a house to stay at nearby. www.hectorpottery.co.nz

Just north of Ngakawau, at Hector, is David Bridger's *Old Slaughterhouse*, worth the climb — a 10-minute walk up the hillside — for cosy backpacker accommodation and a fantastic view. David, whose mother Bub wrote the wonderful poem on page 6, will take your bags up for you on the quad bike. It's comfortable and companionable — there are resident Labradors, decks everywhere, and a large communal area with everything you need to cook your own food or relax with a book from the shelves. Dean Creek, RD1, Hector, (03) 782 8333. The sunsets are free; you can buy food nearby at the very laidback *Drifters Café*, down at Granity.

Our old friend Gay Sweeney, who hosted us out of Greymouth on an earlier trip, now owns the aptly named *Charming Creek B&B*. She didn't invent the name either — the property is on the edge of the Charming Creek Walkway. You can even soak in a driftwood-fired hot tub on the edge of the ocean. (03) 782 8007, www.bullerbeachstay.co.nz

The Karamea Bluffs should offer spectacular views, but were totally fogged in when we made our trip, and it seemed to take forever to get to the *Beachfront Farmstay B&B*, a haven where we spent a pleasant night and enjoyed local whitebait with fresh bread for breakfast. Dianne and Russell Anderson are the third generation of dairy farmers on the property; she's a quilter too. You can drive your trusty rental right up to the door of the quiet wing, where a spacious, comfortable bed befitting a boutique hotel awaits. Arrange in advance to join them for an evening meal with organic vegetables, homemade dessert and New Zealand wine — and if you're not sold yet, check Dianne's blog for taste temptations. Or take your chances at the pub in Karamea, where we had some overcooked — but still delicious — whitebait patties. (03) 782 6762, www.westcoastbeachaccommodation.co.nz

Karamea's former artist-in-residence, dollmaker Helen Back, has migrated to Bluff with her family — read about her new gallery, Jimmi Rabbitz, in the Otago and Southland chapter (see page 249).

South of Greymouth, Hokitika — already the butt of many puns — now has a quilt shop of its own, 6 km north of town at Kaihinu (look for the main-road sign), which cleverly picks up on the Kiwi expression made famous by pioneer TV game-show host Selwyn Toogood half a century ago. Michele Armstrong opened *By Hoki Quilts* — co-owned with her husband Jon, the local community constable ('He's the one who puts up with threads and fabric scattered throughout our home') — in their basement garage in 2007; a woodburner keeps it toasty in winter and wisteria provides shade in summer. Michele focuses on quality solids or fabric that reads as solid — she has all 60 Australian Leutenegger

Homespuns. She runs UFO (Unfinished Objects) days each second and fourth Sunday, 10am to 4pm. Closed Tuesdays; open 10am to 6pm other weekdays and 10am to 1pm weekends — 'But call and I'll do my darndest to be here,' she says. 100 One Mile Line Road, RD2, (03) 755 8515, www.byhokiquilts.blogspot.com

You can expect some rain on the West Coast — though we had it everywhere on this trip; what a wet spring it was! At Hokitika we experienced the most torrential downpour I've ever encountered, but that didn't stop us grabbing something to eat at the *Tin Shed Gallery and Café*, 89 Revell St, (03) 755 8444, which also had knitting by local good keen bloke John Rattray. Clutching our brolly all the while, we crossed the road to a hospice shop with lots of bits and pieces to make a job-lot offer on.

Hokitika is the greenstone capital of New Zealand and you can see it, buy it or even try working it at several places in the town — check out jadecountry.co.nz. *Hokitika Craft Gallery*, a cooperative at 25 Tancred St, has quality work by the region's artisans, including silk dyer Janice Harnett, knitter Alison Tibbles and weaver Helen Oliver, whose work includes the softest baby blankets. (03) 755 8802, www.hokitikacraftgallery.co.nz

You'll be ready for a comfort stop by the time you reach Pukekura in South Westland — population two — halfway between Greymouth and Franz Josef. Prize-winning possum pies and hats and other great gear made from oilcloth and possum skins by fashion graduate Justine (Bowyangs is her label) are just part of the fun at The Bushman's Centre. You can stay a night and dine on road kill — they say they're just joking! — at Justine and Pete's place on either side of the main highway,

35 minutes south of Hokitika. Unfortunately, an earthquake caused the hot pools to spring a leak so they may not be available when you read this. (03) 755 4144, www.pukekura.co.nz

Further south on the main road as you pass through Harihari is *The Willows*, a charming old board-and-batten cottage where Dutch-born spinner and knitter Nolly Martini has for 26 years sold a wide range of crafts including handspun knitwear of all sizes and colours. (Real name Arnolda — 'I was the youngest of 12 girls and they ran out of girls' names and called me after my Uncle Arnold!') We stopped here in pouring rain, and if we hadn't been so wet would definitely have tried on some of the soft and cuddly jerseys. (03) 753 3167.

.

Snazzy Snail Mail

Upcycled envelopes from vintage maps and other paper goodness

Choose firm glossy or matt paper to recycle — old atlas pages, sheet music, gardening books, magazines or calendar pages. Generally these used to be printed on wonderful firm paper – excellent for recycling! The page should be at least A4 size. Keep in mind that your final front surface will probably be on an angle.

Following the sketch, make a template to a size that fits your chosen paper. Place the envelope template with the broader top flap into the left-hand corner of the paper. Trace around the template with a pencil. Now, cut out the shape smoothly.

Score and fold the lines between the four outside flaps, then fold inwards. Use a glue stick to run a 1-cm-wide line of glue down each lower side of the side flaps. Fold the large lower flap upwards, then press it down to the side flaps and smooth it with your thumb.

An adhesive computer address label can be used to make a clear space to address a letter. Try heart-shaped plain stickers, or even cut your own simple shape and glue it on.

Use a glue stick on the inside top flap to secure.

And . . . Voila! Snazzy Snail Mail.

DESIGNED BY: SUE WHITBURN OF FRESH VINTAGE, 49 CARNELL ST, NAPIER

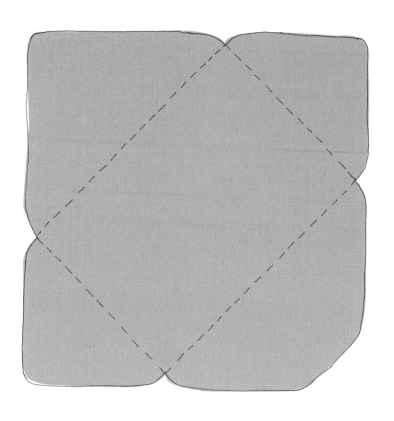

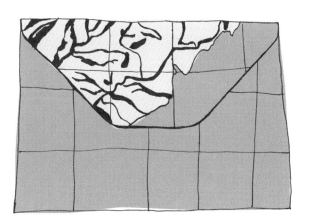

Things
to Make
and Do

Chapter Nine

CANTERBURY

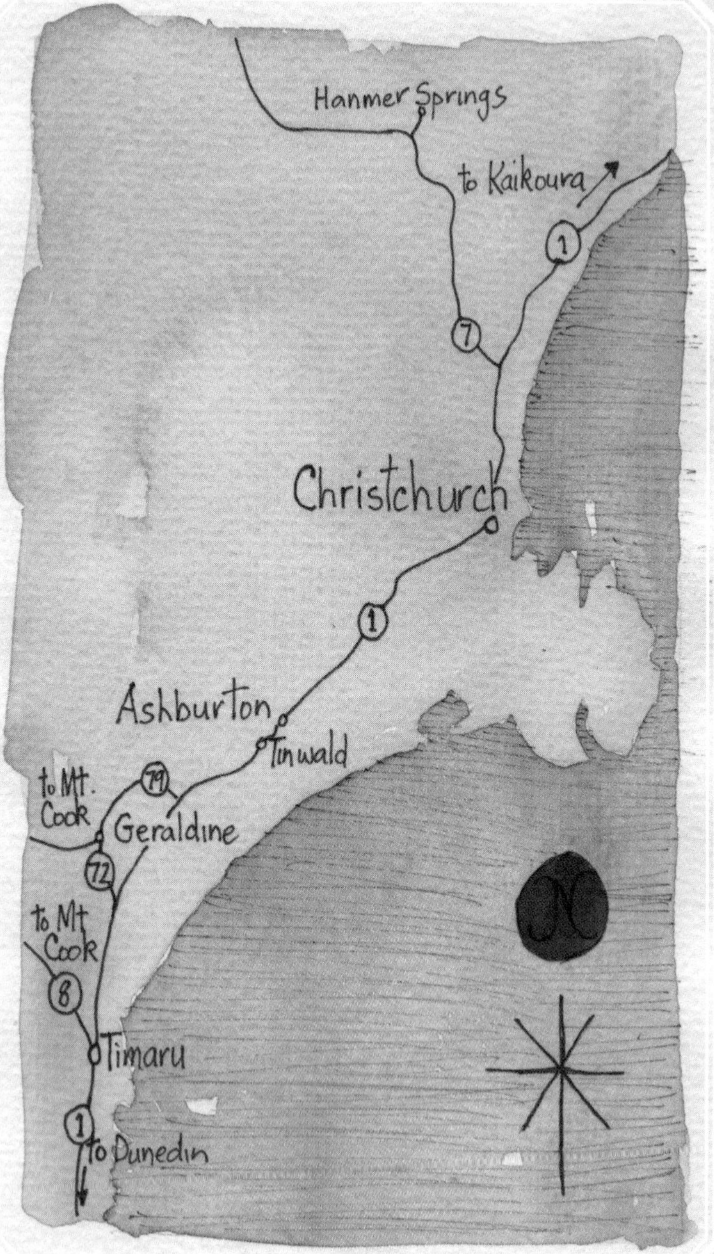
Hanmer Springs
to Kaikoura
1
7
Christchurch
1
Ashburton
Tinwald
79
to Mt. Cook
Geraldine
72
to Mt Cook
8
Timaru
1
to Dunedin

To rewrite Christchurch could take as long as the rebuilding process — that's too long. But those resilient Cantabrians who have stayed in the city are bouncing back after an excess of earthquakes, and are selling their wares in borrowed spaces, pop-up shops and newly formed weekend markets.

They're gathering in friends' homes, church halls and undamaged commercial premises to stitch together and share survival stories. And they're slowly rebuilding their lives and their businesses. Coffee roasteries are becoming the gathering places in many suburbs.

In spring, when I visited — one year on from the first shock — the magnolias were magnificent. Daffodils shone under the trees in Hagley Park and people took advantage of beautiful weather to congregate wherever there was a coffee shop or outdoor event. It's a treat to come across old buildings with character, lifting spirits starved of architectural heritage.

The weekend the All Blacks came to town, a local team rescued the craft fair abandoned by Australian interests and brought together merchants from all over the South Island in a successful Creative Flair Fair which promises to be an annual event. Crafty types turned out in droves on the sunny weekend to take in three quilt exhibitions as well as a broad range of craft offerings, from patchwork to scrapbooking, at Riccarton Racecourse.

The city's arts hub has gone — for now anyway. At the time of writing, the stunning *Christchurch Art Gallery, Te Puna o Waiwhetu*, was still being used as the headquarters for Civil Defence's recovery operations and the restaurant was closed. But the excellent gallery shop was still open.

The historic Arts Centre, located in the heart of town in the Gothic Revival buildings that were the original home of Canterbury College and more recently home to many artists, was severely damaged by the February quake. Those artists and artisans with the heart to carry on are setting up at home, in borrowed studios, or in premises further out of town.

Weaver *Anne Field*, one of many who lost their Arts Centre studios in the quake, is now working from her home in Christchurch— but you'll need to email first. afield@chch.planet.org.nz. www.annefield.co.nz

Some art and craft stallholders from the former weekend market at the Arts Centre are selling at the outdoor *Sunday Artisan Market* at Riccarton House & Bush. 16 Kahu Rd, Riccarton, (03) 348 6190, sundayartisanmarket.co.nz. That's where I met spinner and knitter *Rosemary Rattray*, who keeps a small flock of black and coloured sheep on land around her railway cottage at Ethelton Valley, a few kilometres south of Cheviot. She and her daughter Jocelyn Rattray sat spinning in the sunshine on a beautiful spring day, adding to the stock of finely knitted beanies, ponchos, mittens and hoodies that were on sale. Most are in natural wool colours but there's also a selection of baby beanies with subtle and safe dyes produced from jelly crystals — a new one on me! Railway Cottage Woollenz, (03) 319 8001, 022 687 8329.

It doesn't come much more local than this — Ken Blakemore makes fine lambskin gloves and baby slippers as well as farming deer at his farm *Manaburn* at Okuku, near Rangiora. 950 Birch Hill Rd, RD4, (03) 312 8764.

Bookbinder *Peter Melville* uses possum, deer and goat skins to bind his heritage notebooks, journals and one-off versions of books by landscape photographers like Andris Apse and Craig Potton. 340 Falvey Rd, RD4, Timaru, (03) 614 7644, www.offtheroadbooks.com

I bought one of Carol Boe's elegant *Hollywell* velvet and lavender eye bags, which she sells along with wheat packs and pretty patterned doorstops while also looking after her daughter's fragrant range of Blue Earth soaps and oils. 47 Holly Rd, St Albans, (03) 355 9158.

In a former life *Penelope Hester-Roe*, now a farmer's wife, cook and B&B owner, was a model. Her sense of style shows in the duckdown-filled cotton and velvet cushions she embroiders with favourite literary quotes. You can commission a cushion featuring your own words or choose one of her classy stock pieces to enliven your favourite chair. (03) 329 0095, www.homesteadlinens.co.nz

Award-winning tapestry weaver Marilyn Rea-Menzies lost her *Christchurch Tapestry Workshop* in the Arts Centre but nevertheless managed to finish her latest project, a screen commissioned by Susan, Lady Satyanand, as a farewell gift to Government House in Wellington. Follow her progress at www.tapestry.co.nz/blog/

Also in Riccarton, which was not so badly affected by the quakes, Margaret Haverland has renamed her store *The Art of Sewing* to better reflect what she and her experienced staff are trying to share. She offers classes and also stocks Janome machines. 98 Division St,
(03) 348 0170, www.artofsewing.co.nz

Ballantynes — a Christchurch institution for an astonishing 150 years — decamped in style to their Timaru store before reopening in a somewhat smaller CBD store at the end of October 2011. In the interim, they transported — and entertained — busloads of Christchurch shoppers and staff twice a week to less shaky temporary premises two hours south.
0800 656 400, www.ballantynes.com

Papanui has a good little cluster of crafty shops. Bronwyn Harper doubled her store size by relocating her *Bernina Sewing Centre* to 466 Papanui Rd, (03) 366 8916, in an area largely unaffected by the quake. There's carparking at the rear and right next door the charming *Rosy Antiques & Café*, which also sells old china and other collectables. Your tea is served in pretty vintage cups from real teapots and the food is good value. Couches in the window offer a chance to relax while you take stock. 466c Papanui Rd, (03) 354 5300.

Just along the road at 505A is a tiny wool and bead shop called *The Bead Hive*, (03) 354 8657.

Around the kink in Papanui Road is *Fabric Vision* — their CBD store has closed and this multi-striped store (parking off the busy road) now boasts a vibrant mix of craft fabric, dressmaking yardage in the newest gorgeous florals, loads of haberdashery and buttons and quite a bit of bargain fabric too. 39 Main North Rd, (03) 354 8361, www.fabricvision.co.nz

Who hasn't heard of Ashfords? The Ashburton-based firm revived spinning and weaving way back in the 1930s — which makes them nearly 80 years old. Their popular Traditional wheel introduced a generation of crafty Kiwi women to spinning in the sixties, and the business still operates out of Ashburton. If you can't get there to visit their craft village, you'll be pleased to know the *Hands Ashford* store at 5 Normans Rd, Elmwood, survived the quakes. The shop still overflows with a 'diverse and vast array' of handcraft supplies, as their catalogue puts it. They've got books, classes, tools and raw ingredients for just about anything you might want to have a go at, from beads, books and bears to soap and candlemaking products, papercrafts, all the usual fibre crafts, plus not-so-common pursuits like quilling and pergamano (painting and embossing on parchment). Breezy young assistant manager Sarah Chisnall loves needle felting. 'There's nothing hi-tech about it, it's cheap and boys love it! It's also a fantastic way to darn holes in jerseys.' Closed Sundays and statutory holidays. (03) 355 9099, www.handscraftstore.com

Broomfields Fine Needle Work Supplies, now owned by Andrea Dell, still sells beautiful kits and everything to embroider with, but the quake forced a move from the CBD — where it had moved from Merivale — to Riccarton. It's just off Deans Ave by the Riccarton roundabout, at 76 Brockworth Place. Closed Sundays and Mondays. (03) 377 2748, broomfields.co.nz

There's another *Bernina* centre at Miller's Home World, 367 Blenheim Rd in Upper Riccarton, (03) 348 5159. And old-established cut-price fabric warehouse *Kutwell Fabrics Ltd* has reopened at 580 Colombo St, (03) 366 4093, www.kutwellfabrics.co.nz

Christchurch still has plenty of wool shops. *Knit World*'s Christchurch store is their biggest, and it didn't suffer too much damage in the quakes so it's back up and running; it may even boast a café by the time you read this. Part of a chain of 10 specialist shops around the country — I've listed most regionally — it's located half a dozen blocks from the casino, at 189 Peterborough St. (03) 379 2300, www.knitting.co.nz

Addington is slowly coming back to life, focused around the unmissable *Addington Coffee Co-op*, housed in an earthquake-strengthened former mechanics' workshop at 297 Lincoln Rd. Very Fair Trade, they are, from the roastery producing their signature Jail Breaker coffee from ethically sourced beans ('so good it should be illegal') to the organic cotton T-shirts and bags from FreeSet, the New Zealand-sponsored Kolkata collective that provides employment for former prostitutes. The food's great too, there's parking out the back and plenty of outdoor seating. Open seven days from 7.30am weekdays, 9am weekends, (03) 934 1662, www.addingtoncoffee.org.nz

Across the road in a small shopping centre is a big *Sallies* store, to aid your op shop itch. There's still a *Knitters' Factory Shop* in Addington Mall, 300 Lincoln Road, (03) 338 7110. See the links page for an Australasian website which lists more.

Also out at Addington, in what was once a Methodist church hall — and a table tennis venue — *The Painted Room* ('purveyors of fine oddities') shares premises with *Era* antiques in a venerable old interior. (Don't be fooled by the spiky fence and dark grey stucco exterior.) Offered the space just three days after the February quake, colleagues Caren Butler, her business partner Brigid Ryan and collector Julian Hobday say they just had to get stuck in and set up shop again. Caren's unexpected combinations of fabric and fur come to life beneath over 300 of Julian's trademark chandeliers. Everything has a story — walk in and smile at inside-out, patched fur coats; cushions combining worn Sanderson loose covers, BNZ banking bags and old Union Jacks; and fabric-coated repainted furniture. 'Maximum style, minimum waste' is Caren's motto — and she swears there are no barcodes. Closed Sundays and

Mondays. 407 Selwyn St, cnr Harmon St,
(03) 366 3967, 021 922 039 (Caren), 027 358 2214
(Julian).

 Diagonally across the road is *Hummingbird Coffee*'s
roastery and the splendid *Oddfellows Café*, in
another lovely old interior — a former lodge hall.
Take your time to enjoy the fab food and
ambience. Off-street parking. 5 Disraeli St,
(03) 377 6757.

Across the city, doll's-house and miniature
collectors will find *Enchanted Garden Dolls Houses*,
the backyard studio where Linda Laurenson has
been making and selling her tiny treasures for
over 18 years. She has a full range of everything
you need from the house itself — she reckons
her prices can't be beaten! — to wallpapers
and furniture. Enchanting indeed. Open by
appointment. 58 Perth St, Richmond,
(03) 366 2822, enchantedgarden@clear.net.nz

 Jackie Nicholls designs American and French
Country style folk art patterns, under her label
House on the Hill, from her home at 25 Konini St,
Fendalton, where she also teaches classes. You can
buy her immaculately detailed small wooden
painted and textile houses, hearts and other
goodies in many parts of the country — and in
France and Italy too. Her patterns are easy to
follow — we've included one on page 26. Visitors
are welcome at home but strictly by appointment.
(03) 348 2361, www.houseonthehill.co.nz

 Out at Woolston there's a splendid antiques centre
that brings together eight dealers including Sue
Wootton, of *Warehorne Antiques and Collectibles*,
who's always on the lookout for old textiles. We met
by chance at Jimpy's in Nelson, when we were both
going through his soft stuff, so a visit to *Ferry*

Antique Centre was a must. They lost the back part of their old building (now cordoned off) but the front is a storehouse for collectors of everything from Victorian to retro objects, small furniture pieces and china. I went away with retro wallpaper and the sweetest little Swiss linen hankie, bordered with embroidered edelweiss and gentians. 598 Ferry Rd, (03) 376 4016. Sue Wootton: (03) 348 0444.

Before I could concentrate on the goodies on offer, however, I needed reviving, so Sue sent me down the block to the stunning heritage building that houses award-winning *Holy Smoke* café, deli and restaurant. They cater for everyone from local mums relaxing with their babies in a sunny window to full-scale fine-dining customers — and writers in search of caffeine. Love their Terry Stringer sculptures, too. Check out their great website. Closed public holidays. 650 Ferry Rd, (03) 943 2222, www.holysmoke.co.nz

Not far away is Marjan and Peter Glamuzina's toy shop *Spindlewood*, at 14 Brabourne St, Hillsborough. Committed Steiner folk, they stock toys, finger puppets, handcrafted dolls, puzzles, games, dress-ups and candles and all sorts of natural goodies — many of which they make themselves. (03) 960 9777, www.spindlewood.co.nz

On the way out there is scrapbooking supplier *Rubber Stamps by Montarga* at 165 Ferry Rd, just off Fitzgerald Ave. Closed Sundays. (03) 366 9963, www.montarga.co.nz

Spotlight's Christchurch store, open seven days, is on the corner of Colombo and Elgin Sts in Sydenham. (03) 377 6121, www.spotlight.co.nz

Legendary fabric shop *Bolt of Cloth* has reopened after the quake in bright new premises at Colombo Mall, 363 Colombo St, Sydenham. Open seven days, (03) 341 5070, www.boltofcloth.com

Christchurch lost thousands of hotel beds in the quakes, and some bed and breakfast establishments also suffered. So as one who prefers the personal touch of a B&B to other kinds of accommodation, I was delighted when Jan and Alan Taylor at *Belmont Bed and Breakfast* offered to host me in the Shaky City. As well as a comfortable bed in a villa that's survived all the big quakes virtually unscathed, I had a desk to write at, good breakfasts each morning and a relaxed lounge to wind down in at the end of the day. I can't believe the hours Alan keeps — he'll happily pick up inbound tourists from the airport in the middle of the night and drop them out to meet 4am international check-ins. Could be the years he spent as a firefighter … which is certainly reassuring during occasional wee aftershocks. 37 Harewood, Papanui, (03) 354 6890, www.belmontbnb.co.nz

There's a good Thai restaurant, *Phuket*, a short walk away at 513 Papanui Rd, (03) 352 8507.

My favourite Christchurch ethnic restaurant is the much-loved *Bodhi Tree*, which has now opened again in larger premises in Fendalton. If you've not tasted Burmese cuisine, it's quite different from the ethnic flavours we're more used to — intriguing taste combinations, a good wine list and impeccable service make this a place to seek out. If their message says they're booked out, try anyway — they've squeezed us in on more than one occasion. 399 Ilam Rd, (03) 377 6808.

In the same block of shops is the tantalising *Villa Antiques*, with a breathtaking mix of old stuff from

the traditionally elegant to the functional — well-oiled vintage garden tools, for example. I couldn't resist a quartet of brightly coloured retro sundae dishes. 401A Ilam Rd, Fendalton, (03) 351 5644, www.villa.antiques.co.nz

Hornby, on the edge of the city as you head south, has two places for crafty girls. Daphne Barker's *Barkers Wool & Haberdashery*, at 9 Witham St, (03) 349 7867, has everything for knitters as well as Pfaff sewing machines. Cheryl McDowell of *Needle Arts*, at Unit 2, 58 Carmen Rd, leans to the French and European style in her embroidery and quilting ranges, and takes in beading to be repaired by Made By Me in Rolleston (see page 210). (03) 344 5235, www.needlearts.co.nz

Scrapbooking is still big in Christchurch. Hilary Nicholas set up *Scrap it Simple* at home two years ago at 39A Chipping Lane, Redwood, finding scrapbooking to be a healing process after the death of her mother. Hilary takes classes during the week and is open Mondays to Fridays 10am to 1pm, as well as Tuesday and Thursday afternoons 3.30 to 5.30pm. (03) 354 5101, www.scrapitsimple.co.nz

Fresh, light and modern, *Stitch*, 'the playroom for knitters and stitchers', lifts your spirits from the moment you step through the door. After the quakes — never mind that the house she'd just finished renovating after moving south from Auckland was in ruins — Penny Jameson and her daughter Fenella threw their shop open to anyone who wanted to come in and sew. Free classes gave everybody the chance to tell their stories, and coffee sessions continue to bring the community together. Tucked under the Cashmere Hills, Penny and Fenella bring a contemporary fabric-based approach to quilting, with ranges from bright young things like Saffron Craig to the eternally youthful Kaffe Fassett. There's a playroom for kids too, and gorgeous wools — from Debbie Bliss to locally hand-dyed yarns. Husqvarna dealers. (03) 332 1820, www.stitchplayroom.com

Lynn Norman, a folk-art painter and long-time maker of cloth dolls, set up her *Cottonfields Quilting Quarters* — pun intended, I'm sure — just three years ago after running classes from home and selling at events such as the Culverden Fair over many years. As you'd expect from the name, her purpose-built store at 45 Merrin Street, Avonhead, has a country flavour. Closed Sundays, public holidays and public holiday weekends. (03) 358 3355, www.cottonfields.co.nz

North of Christchurch city, on the main road at Belfast, is *Jolene's Web*, the trading name for Joanne Bryce and Raelene Wiersma's shop at 812 Main North Rd. They stock supplies for quilters and other crafters and are the agents for Elna machines. (03) 323 4311.

Down the Plains to Timaru

Heading down the flat, flat Canterbury Plains can be quite soporific. It's interesting to pop off the long straight road into tiny towns that still have heritage buildings standing — unlike many parts of Christchurch.

If you feel the need to bead, call into Rolleston's *Made By Me*, to the right of the main road at Unit 1, 817 Jones Rd. Vicki Allen and friends Sylvia Masson and Penny Fanshawe offer readymade

jewellery plus workshops in every aspect of creating wearable accessories from beads in their space. (03) 347 3570, www.madebyme.co.nz

A great all-round crafty stop is *Ashford Village*, an hour south of Christchurch on the main road at Ashburton. *Knitcola Stitchery*, formerly Ashford Craft Shop and Museum, and home to the world's most famous modern spinning wheel, is based in the 100-year-old Mill House, built for the owner of a neighbouring flour mill. New owner Nicola Bota has revamped the interior to include a relaxed studio space for all-comers — including you, dear reader — to have a play with the wealth of yarns, spinning wheels, needles and other gear on sale. Nicola's mother Lois — the inspiration behind her daughter's takeover of the old family business — is probably knitting up a storm behind the counter. They also offer craft retreats. These days there's lots more wool for knitters but they still display the raw stuff for spinners at the heart of the house. The museum has an extensive collection of spinning wheels from around the world, including the original Ashford spinning wheel made by founder Walter Ashford in 1940. When you've had your fill of play, there's sustenance at hand in the café under the same roof. Plenty of off-street parking. Open seven days and most public holidays. 427 West St (Highway 1), (03) 308 9085, www.ashfordcraftshop.co.nz

The line-up circled around a village green includes a craft cooperative, *Amelia's* — vintage chic and nice things — and Ashburton's *Bernina Sewing Centre*, on the main road on your right coming into town at 435 West St. (03) 308 6570.

Watch for Rachel Anne Maw's vintage gold VW parked on the road when you cross the Ashburton River going south. Tinwald is the oldest part of Ashburton, across the river from the rest of town, and *Annie's Country Quilt Store* is housed in a 100-year-old pioneer cottage which has now been refreshed after suffering earthquake damage. How Rachel managed to move and replace all that stock is beyond me! Antiques and collectables add charm to room after room of patchwork fabric and kits (check out the locker hooking samples), DMC cotton, gifts and patterns sourced internationally — and Rachel adds at least one sample to her stock each week to go out with her weekly email newsletter. Judged runner-up for Ashburton's Top Shop in 2011, this is still one of the South Island's best finds, drawing a lot of passing tourist traffic as well as quilters who come for weekly, evening and one-off weekend project classes. The jug is always on for a cuppa. Open seven days. 167 Archibald St (main road), (03) 307 6277, www.anniesquilts.co.nz

Rachel's a passionate advocate for her home town. She recommends the nearby *Lake House* restaurant and bar at the alpine-fed Lake Hood — perhaps the region's best-kept secret, with its international rowing course, among other features — for an unsurpassed water's edge refreshment stop. Open from 10am seven days, (03) 302 6064, www.lakehood.co.nz. For the blokes, there's *The Plains Vintage Railway & Historical Museum*, just off State Highway 1 in Maronan Rd, Tinwald, www.plainsrailway.co.nz, and the *Ashburton Aviation Museum* at Ashburton Airport. Open by arrangement. (03) 308 6408.

Further south, at Orari, is the turnoff to Geraldine, a pretty country town with a pleasant park at its heart and an old-fashioned independent movie

theatre that screens all sorts of classics. Geraldine is perhaps best known as the home of Barkers' fruit products — the family firm is now over 40 years old. They're still at the large *Berry Barn Complex* on the corner of Cox and Talbot Sts, along with a café and Alpaca Centre. (03) 693 7363.

Lacemaker and weaver Jean Lillia Hall and her husband have retired to Geraldine, where she still welcomes visitors, by arrangement, to *Lillia's Lace Museum* — named after her lacemaking grandmother and previously in Lower Moutere, out of Nelson. 240A Talbot St, Geraldine. Jean also handpaints lace bobbins for collectors. (03) 693 9312, www.homepages.paradise.net.nz/flaxland/

There could hardly be a better advertisement for a wool business than a listing in the *Guinness Book of Records*. Geraldine is home to the legendary machine-knitting business *The Giant Jersey* in Wilson St, named for the enormous sample woolly that's their brand. They sell a range of knitted jumpers to match. There's also a mosaic of spring steel recreating the Bayeux Tapestry. Unbelievable! (03) 693 9820, www.giantjersey.co.nz

Betty Twaddle's patchwork haven *Needle 'n' Thread* has an extensive range of fabric including flannels — appropriate given this is the gateway to the mountains — plus haberdashery. Her limited-edition nativity advent calendar has been reprinted following popular demand. Open normal business hours, (03) 693 1122, or email betty.needlenthread@gmail.com

On the main highway at Temuka, north of Timaru, you'll see obsessive quilter Sue Dwyer's bright yellow *Obsession 2 Quilt* shop right on the main road. 239 King St, (03) 615 6232, www.obsession2quilt.co.nz

Timaru's town centre is much bigger than I remember it — and I managed to get lost in the suburbs on my way out before finding the main road again with the help of my trusty iPhone. The older part of town has been integrated with the main street shops and new government buildings and it's much more interesting than it used to be.

The town is a mecca for op shopping — check out the side streets: I found five, and I know there are more, because the lively Linda Butler at the bustling *Timaru Sewing Centre* worked out a list for me. Linda sells Janome machines and has a one-stop-shop stock of every fabric variety — patchwork, ballgown, dress and craft — plus knitting wools. She runs classes too, at 173 Stafford St. (03) 688 6764, www.timarusewing.co.nz

Pam's Patch & Needlecraft has been part of the local craft scene for 21 years. Pam and Robin Fuller's shop at 214 Stafford St stocks the usual patchwork and embroidery fabric, notions and knitting wool. Open normal shopping hours. (03) 688 3248.

In Church St there's a Presbyterian op shop across the road from Charmaine Shand's *Demco Wool & Sewing Centre*; (03) 688 0846. And for knitters there's the specialist wool shop *Knit Purl*, in Woollcombe St, (03) 684 5890.

Timaru has some good antique shops too — Joy Giles' *Serendipity Antiques* is still at 45a Stafford St, on the way into town from the south. Last trip I found special pieces of vintage dressmaking fabric and haberdashery that had come from an estate and there were lots of other treasures worth spending time over. (03) 688 0498, joygiles@xtra.co.nz

Twizel

Shiree Johnston is living her dream — opening a quilt shop in one of the most stunningly beautiful parts of the country. She and her GP husband and family moved to the former hydro town some years ago so the kids, keen rowers, could have access to Lake Ruataniwha — is the shop's name, *The Rowan Tree Quilt Gallery & Workshop*, a pun perhaps? Shiree started her quilting career as a long-arm quilter then decided she could have a shop too. It's an extension of her home and her studio is behind it, so she'll put the kettle on for visitors. Generally, says Shiree, the shop is open 'most Tuesdays, all day Wednesday, Friday and Saturday, and sometimes Sundays, 10am-4pm or thereabouts, later if I am busy quilting! Usually I am closed on Mondays, but occasionally I open this day as well.' (03) 435 0359, www.therowantree.co.nz

A Weekend In The Country

Just 90 minutes' drive north from Christchurch, on good roads, Hanmer Springs has been a refuge for tired travellers for over 150 years — and there's a resident textile artist! Hanmer's good all year round but especially pretty in autumn, with towering deciduous trees dropping their leaves on the carpark next to the pools in the heart of town. Locals reckon the best time to soak in the hot pools — there are seven outdoors, including three therapeutic sulphur pools — is when it's snowing. They're certainly at their most photogenic then, along with the surrounding hills; starry nights seem to be part of the deal, too.

A night in the hot springs haven was a treat on our way to Nelson via the Lewis Pass. If you need to stop on the way for food, the award-winning *Nor'Wester Café* in Amberley is a good choice, on the main road north, before the turnoff to Hanmer and the West Coast. It's open seven days for brunch, lunch and dinner.
(03) 314 9411, www.norwestercafe.co.nz

Cheltenham House is a heritage B&B just off the main street in the heart of town — a hop and a skip from the hot pools and the village, where we were spoiled for choice restaurant-wise. Len and Maree Earl, perfect low-key hosts, have lived in the district all their lives and offer exceptional service from drinks in the billiard room before dinner, to breakfast brought to our room in the morning.

Before breakfast, I slid back the windows to expose hidden doors in the sunporch annex of our room, and sneaked out across the garden for a riverbank stroll along nearby Dog Stream walkway, beneath unusually tall deciduous trees just coming into leaf. Then it was back to write up my journal over a cup of tea, before a fabulously full breakfast was brought on a butler's tray to our private haven. 13 Cheltenham St, Hanmer Springs, (03) 315 7545, www.cheltenham.co.nz

The village offers good gift shopping, including *Up The Garden Path*, once housed in a wee cottage now put out to grass in the country. They have a good selection of handwoven silks, candles and massage oils, and a range of gifts for all ages, including children. 5 Conical Hill Rd, (03) 315 7915.

Since the last edition of *Crafty Girls*, Grace Down has closed her quilt business, nature park and café. But textile artist and educator *Jane Van Keulen*, well known for her fabulous threads, has made the move from Kaiapoi to Hanmer's Charwell Lodge, where she continues to offer sumptuous embroidered items, hand-dyed threads, beads, and contemporary embroidery kits, as well as workshops. Turn right on the way into town, up a road leading to a site with spectacular views that are sure to inspire.
82 Medway Rd, (03) 315 5070, www.janevk.com

If you're travelling on to Nelson, think about stopping at *Maruia Springs* for a special experience. Indeed, you may be the only guests in one of the three rocky, au naturel hot pools. The view across the river to bush-covered hills is magical — and well worth the hire charge if you haven't brought your own towel. There's a Japanese bath-house and you can eat Japanese cuisine and stay here too. Highway 7, Lewis Pass, (03) 523 8840, www.maruiasprings.co.nz

Winter Booties

to fit age: 0–3 m, 3–6 m, 6–12 m
(2nd and 3rd sizes are shown in brackets)

MATERIALS
1 ball of 8 ply yarn
One pair each of 3.25 mm and 4 mm needles

TENSION
22 sts and 28 rows to 10 cm on
4 mm needles over stocking stitch

ABBREVIATIONS
K = knit, P = purl, rep = repeat,
rem = remaining, inc = increase, tog = together,
cont = continue, alt = alternate, st(s) = stitch(es),
tbl = through back of loop

BOOTEES
(Knit 2 alike)
Commence at the centre of the sole.
Using 4 mm needles, cast on 27 (33, 39) sts.
1st and following 3 alt rows: K
2nd row: K1, inc in next st, K10 (13, 16), inc, K1, inc, K10 (13, 16) inc, K1
4th row: K1, inc, K12 (15, 18), inc, K1, inc, K12 (15, 18) inc, K1
6th row: K1, inc, K14 (17, 20), inc, K1, inc, K14 (17, 20), inc, K1
8th row: K1, inc, K16 (19, 22), inc, K1, inc, K16 (19, 22), inc, K1. 43 (49, 55) sts
Knit 5 (7, 9) rows
Instep shaping
1st row: K24 (28, 30), K2tog tbl, turn
2nd row: (K1, P1) 2 (3, 3) times, K1, P2tog, turn
3rd row: (P1, K1) 2 (3, 3) times, P1, K2 tog tbl, turn
4th row: (K1, P1) 2 (3, 3) times, K1, P2 tog tbl, turn
Repeat last 2 rows until 31 (33, 37) sts remain
Next row: (P1, K1) 2 (3, 3) times, P1, K2tog tbl, knit to end.
Change to 3.25 mm needles

Next row: K0 (0, 1), (P1, K1) 8 (9, 10) times, P2 tog,
*K1, P1, rep from * to last stitch, K0 (0, 1) 29 (31, 35) sts
Continue as set in rib until 19 (21, 21) rows have been worked.
Cast off in rib.

TO MAKE UP
Join the back seam using ladder stitch on wrong side of work,
neatly changing to the other side near the bottom of the ribbing.
This allows the neat side to show when the top is turned over.
Join the heel and sole seam using a flat seam.
Turn top over.

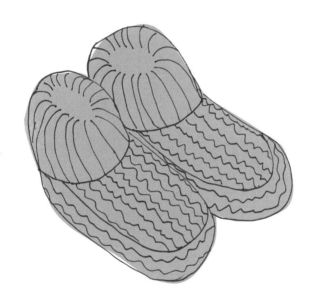

Chapter Ten

DUNEDIN, CENTRAL OTAGO AND SOUTHLAND

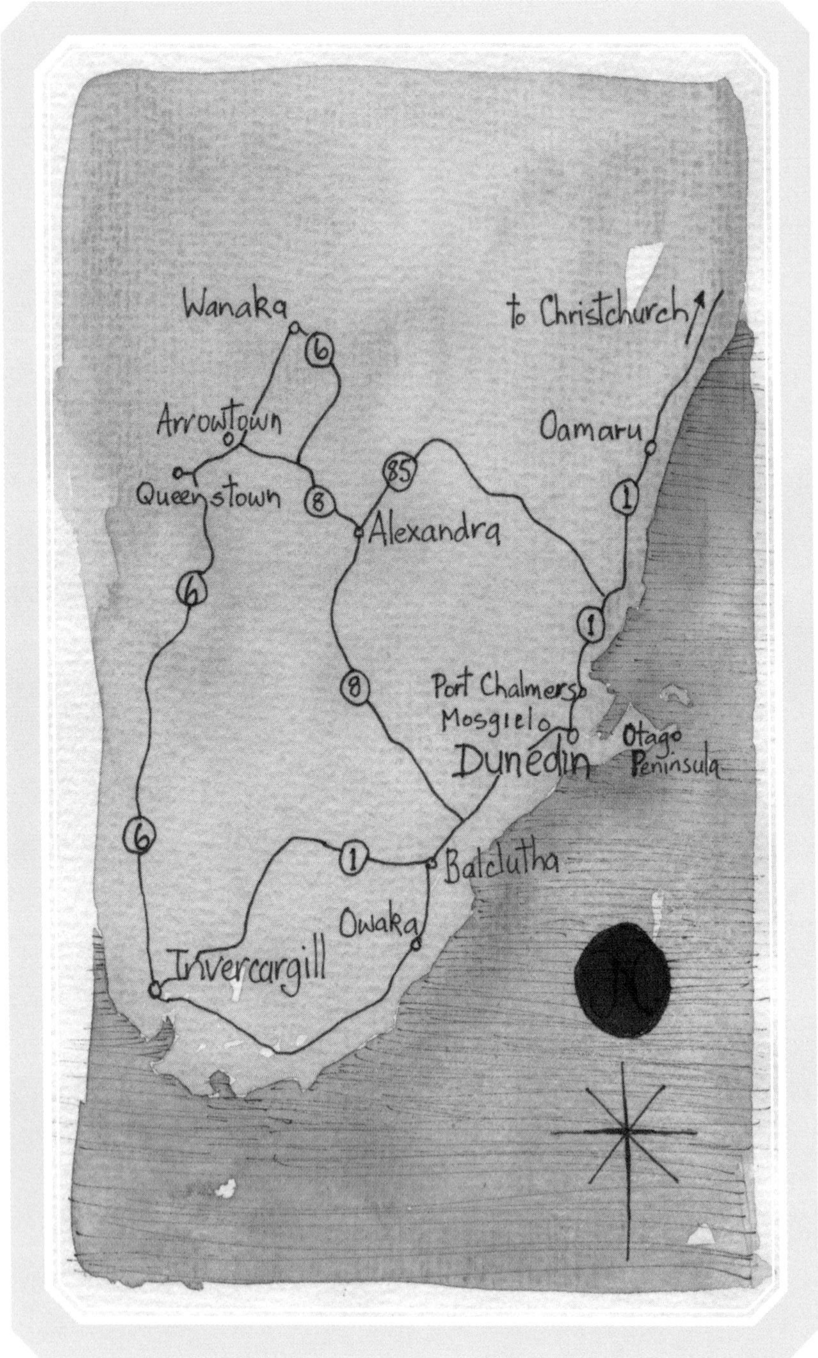

Wanaka
to Christchurch
Arrowtown
Queenstown
Oamaru
85
8
6
1
Alexandra
Port Chalmers
Mosgiel
Otago Peninsula
Dunedin
Balclutha
Owaka
Invercargill
N

The Edinburgh of the south, Dunedin is full of astonishing brick and stone architecture, often perched on steep streets, with spectacular views towards the more rural Otago Peninsula. You can stay overnight at some of these houses, which are boutique B&Bs.

The town belt provides a green backdrop to the city centre and many shops still sport classic leadlight windows and proper entrances where you can shelter from the icy winter blasts that locals simply call 'weather'. The country's earliest university city, Dunedin is easy to get around by car — except when those steep streets ice up in mid-winter, or snow closes the Northern Motorway. We struck extremely wet weather and found the steep hill streets a little daunting — but made it safely to our lodgings. The town has lots of short-term parking which is policed by wardens on motorbikes — don't go away and forget where you've left the car or you could get a ticket.

Though there's no longer an Otago Arts Guide, here are plenty of brochures available at the airport, the information centre or in hotels that feature Dunedin's cultural delights — a detailed guide showing where everything is on the Otago Peninsula, leaflets on the city's many heritage buildings, and information on *Passion for Fashion* experiences, which offer an insider's guided tour of shops and workrooms plus coffee and wine. You can have a jewellery tour too. (03) 478 0610, www.walkthetalk.co.nz

And if you identify with the Scottishness of it all — a sculpted Robert Burns looks out over The Octagon, back to the kirk and face to the tavern — check out *The Scottish Shop*, a block north of The Octagon, at 17 George St; (03) 477 9965, scottishshop.co.nz. You can also have a kilt made by Ann and Richard Corry's *Helean Kiltmakers*, a business that began in 1901. 8 Hocken St, Kenmure, (03) 453 0233, www.dunedin-direct.co.nz/heleankilts

The *Otago Settlers Museum*, partly housed in the old art deco NZR Road Transport building, often shows selections from its excellent costume archive. There's also a very good Chinese display that shows the history of the goldfields and the part played by Chinese immigrants. Open weekdays, weekends and public holiday afternoons, except Christmas Day and Good Friday. 31 Queens Gardens, (03) 477 5052, www.otago.settlers.museum

The *Dunedin Public Art Gallery* — with angle parking across the road — showcases good contemporary New Zealand art plus significant holdings of historical European art, including Tissot's tartan-clad woman *Waiting for the Train*, which has such a Dunedin look about it. The gallery's shop has some of the best local craft and *Nova Café*, right on the street, is known for good coffee as well as great meals. Gallery open daily except Christmas Day, 10am to 5pm. Nova open till late. 30 The Octagon, (03) 477 4000, www.dunedin.art.museum

I was hugely relieved to find Violet Faigan's thoroughly *Modern Miss* had moved rather than closed. She's now by the Rialto at 21 Upper Moray Pl, next to the *White Room* — which sells great New Zealand design — in the old Oxford Buildings. It's a real find for those who love vintage clothing — including menswear — and fabric. Everything here is from the forties to the seventies, except the amazing Miss Faigan, who has an eye for all that's hot and collectable. I loved the Liberty blouses — she has quite a few but they turn over quickly. She will hire out clothing, shoes and accessories for special occasions too. Closed Sundays, otherwise open from 10.30 daily. 021 118 6740, visit the Modern-Miss-Vintage Facebook page.

Just up the road at 51 Moray Pl, *Collectibles* has nearly new clothing. (03) 477 6259.

Threads — aka *Threads Bernina Needlecrafts* — is about the last place in town where you can still buy patchwork and embroidery fabrics. It's at Centre City Mall on Great King St (you get free parking with your till receipt). Threads also stocks Anchor embroidery threads, knitting wools and some delicious ribbons. (03) 477 4514. *Jan's Patch* has gone online only, as has *The Stitchery*. Jenny Paddon, formerly of Needle 'n' Thread in Geraldine, moved to Dunedin in 2006 and opened a shop specialising in patchwork, stitching and interesting knitting yarns — 'all things yummy in that regard'. In 2009 a 'change-of-lifestyle decision' saw her move into a charming B&B cottage called *The City Sanctuary* at 165 Maitland St, which she runs with her son Jake. She still stitches — of course — but now sells online and offers weekend craft retreats at her home. (03) 474 5002, www.thestitchery.co.nz, www.citysanctuary.co.nz

Dressmakers, however, are still well served in Dunedin, especially when it comes to woollen cloth thick enough to keep your legs warm in the coldest winters. *Anne's Sewing Room*, tucked away in Harvest Court Mall off George St, boasts a fabulous range of sumptuous embroidered evening fabrics, superb wools and lots of winceyette for winter PJs. Anne Lewis also has beautiful ribbons and couture trims and an interesting, non-standard assortment of cottons for patchwork. Open from 9.15am daily, closed Sundays. 218 George St, (03) 477 3650.

For those who like to string their own beads, there's a branch of *The Bead Shop* at 7 The Octagon. (03) 477 7420, www.beadshopnz.com

Sue Todd Antiques and Collectables and *Sue Todd Dolls* are now established at 122 Lower Stuart St, with a big workshop out the back. Her dolls are exquisite, with a timelessness that belies their construction date. Sue sells antique furniture and china to match the style of her dolls and has a rack of dolls' clothes as well. (03) 477 7547.

Sue has also opened *The Store*, specialising in adversiting tin and tin toys, at 7 Factory Rd in Mosgiel. (03) 489 3070.

Ha'pennys, a small shop with some intriguing textiles — bolts of vintage fabric, old linen, clothes and a bank of drawers full of notions like buttons, bows and hat netting — has moved into Sue's old city shop at 401 Princes St. 021 144 4260.

In George St, *Everyday Gourmet* has fabulous stocks of imported food, good coffee and exquisite chocolates brought in from the South Canterbury town of Geraldine. Warm and sunny inside in winter, with tables on the street too, you'll want to stop here before nosing around several nearby shops. (03) 477 2045, www.everydaygourmet.net.nz

Waughs at 460 George St has a comprehensive range of labels like Caroline Sills — you get good wear out of your woollies here — with some more way-out designs downstairs. There are shoes, too, from New Zealand designer Kathryn Wilson. Close by is the good little *Obelisk* interiors store at no. 468 and, at the other end of the scale is *St Vincent de Paul*'s op shop where prices are extremely reasonable — and all in a good cause.

Dunedin has a fantastic independent bookstore in the *University Bookshop*, 378 Great King St. They have a lovely website too. Open daily, but weekend hours shorter. (03) 477 6976, www.unibooks.co.nz

And don't forget *Lure*, which features the best New Zealand contemporary jewellery upstairs at 130 Stuart St. (03) 477 5559, www.craftinfo.org.nz

Katya Gunn is a crafty woman who has a day job as a doctor but stitches in every spare moment. She is besotted by beads and has not only some fabulous examples of the bead embroiderer's art — especially bags — but also a significant stash of teeny imported treasures for you to stitch up. You can visit her workroom at home by appointment. (03) 477 9944, www.lucellan.com

Dr David Bellamy calls the Otago Peninsula the finest example of eco-tourism in the world, and we rather like it too. It's a treat to set off for a (maybe misty) morning out on the peninsula. If you want to go all the way to Taiaroa Head and the *Royal Albatross Colony*, allow an hour to get there. There's a café at the Albatross Centre that's open from 10.30am to 3.30pm; (03) 478 0499. We took the road that winds along the top and down into Portobello, which takes about 45 minutes. Don't rush it — these are winding, narrow roads, albeit sealed — and half the point is to catch the breathtaking views out to sea and down into the harbour. Note, too, that there's no fuel available on the Otago Peninsula, so fill up before you go.

From the top road you can call into *Larnach Castle* — it takes about half an hour to get to the wonderful restored house and gardens, which have an entry fee. You can buy lunches and teas or a picnic to take out into the grounds. Built in 1871, the grand old castle has magnificent carved ceilings, antiques, and of course the views. Open every day from 9am to 5pm, later in summer. (03) 476 1616, www.larnachcastle.co.nz

A different experience is to be found at *Glenfalloch*, a woodland garden on the waterfront road, 15 minutes from town. Spring is an especially beautiful time here, with rhododendrons, azaleas and magnolias flowering among deciduous trees bursting into leaf. There's a potter's studio and gallery with work from 10 artisans in a cottage in the garden, and a café and wine bar that opens between 1 September and 30 April, from 11am to 3.30pm weekdays, 4.30pm weekends. Phone first or check the website, (03) 476 1006, www.glenfalloch.co.nz

Sadly, Ian Robertson and his wife have closed *Clifton Wool 'n' Things* at 877 Highcliff Rd, where splendid stone walls, built in 1863 by Ian's grandfather coralled their coloured sheep.

I have never come across a china shop like *Broad Bay China*, at 13 Waikana St, Broad Bay. We didn't make it out there this trip, but I hear a goodly portion of their antique and collectable china — whole dinner-sets and discontinued lines from Royal Doulton to Masons, Carlton to Crown Lynn — has gone to refurbishing Christchurch homes that lost heirloom collections in the quakes. They also have linens, embroidery workbaskets and needlework tools and supplies as well as kitchenalia, boxes, cutlery and costume jewellery. Sue More's shop is open seven days from September to May, closed Mondays and Tuesdays in winter, or by appointment. Do go there! (03) 478 0067, www.broadbaychina.co.nz

Going North: Oamaru

The little fishing village of Moeraki is a perfect place to spend a night. Check into a cabin at the local motor camp and head off for a walk before having a fantastic fish meal at *Fleurs Place*, across the railway line before the boulder beach; (03) 439 4480. Built from recycled architectural remnants, the restaurant commands a view over what was intended to be the port of north Otago. Fleur had to become a fish dealer just to buy the stuff straight off the boats. We came back for breakfast too, after a good — and cheap — night's sleep at the motor camp.

Oamaru's grand 19th-century limestone wharf buildings were constructed to house the grain and wool that created the area's wealth. Now conservation efforts have resulted in a creative precinct that lures tourists to the coastal Otago town, which is also known for its antiques and as the home of craft bookbinder *Michael O'Brien*, 7 Tyne St, South Hill, (03) 434 9277. It's also the home of Steampunk — 'tomorrow as it used to be'.

The *Grainstore Gallery*, in Smith's Union Store Building in the heart of the precinct, is the exhibition and performance space for a diversity of arts people from sculptors to jewellers. The same building, at 9 Tyne St, is the home of the legendary mask artist *Donna Demente*, who can be visited by appointment; (03) 434 8117. Second-hand bookstores and marvellous organic bread are also on offer.

Oamaru's an interesting place — not all that long ago it was the cheapest city in New Zealand in which to buy a house. It has a walking trail in honour of our greatest novelist, Janet Frame, which includes what she saw as her 're-framed' birthplace at 56 Eden St. And that stone that built the Victorian buildings also produces grass that flavours the award-winning Whitestone Cheese, which you can sample at the *Cheesery Cafe*, 3 Torridge St, www.whitestonecheese.co.nz

The city's newest place to eat is the legendary Fleur Sullivan's (see *Fleurs*, opposite) *Loan and Merc* establishment down at the southern end of the Victorian precinct in a rambling, half-gutted former woolstore, once the home of the New Zealand Loan and Mercantile Company. 'Fleur's Other Place' as it's also known, features a more meaty colonial menu than her Moeraki fish restaurant. You can have just a coffee if you wish, although the bar menu, which bears no resemblance to standard pub counter fare, is well worth perusing. 16–18 Harbour St, (03) 434 9905, www.loanandmerc.co.nz

The historic precinct's a bit dead out of season — especially earlier in the week. It comes alive for the increasing number of festivals celebrating times past — if you're planning a trip, try to coincide with one of those events, particularly the *Victorian Heritage Celebrations*. www.historicoamaru.co.nz

On Tees St, above the historic precinct, spinners will find a cheerful little shop selling spinning wheels and wools, run by a husband and wife team — he has an electrical vintage store two doors away from *Woolez Hand Made* at 14 Tees St, opposite the *St Vincent de Paul* op shop. Closed Sundays. (03) 434 2003.

Back in the main shopping street — also Highway 1 — on the corner of Wear St, is the *Oamaru Silk Centre*. The name's more historical than accurate these days — Graeme Shekelton has had a lifetime in the rag trade, taking over the business his dad established in 1952 at a time when silk really was the fabric of choice. (For more history, check the website.) Graeme still sells dressmaking and bridal material and also has a large range of patchwork fabrics, particularly Kiwiana patterns, and he really knows his stuff, so to speak. 119 Thames St, (03) 434 9184, www.oamarusilkcentre.com

On the main road north there are two reasons to stop leaving town — *Arthur's Antiques & Collectables*, 360 Thames Highway, (03) 437 0053, and a good *Sallies* down at the next corner, both on the left-hand side of the road. There's another Sallies further into town and a *Hospice* shop too, both on the left in the shopping precinct.

Somewhere between Oamaru and Timaru the landscape changes almost imperceptibly — but you know you're in a different part of the country. You leave behind the deciduous shelter belts, trimmed to create beautifully skeletal winter silhouettes in the low sunlight. The feeling the sea's not far away gives way to a more pastoral landscape.

You can take a detour here — isn't that what road trips are all about? — into Waimate. Highway 82 goes on through to Wanaka and Queenstown, or you can then head back to the road to Oamaru and Dunedin. All New Zealand-made knitwear outlet *Waimate Knitwear*, at 25 Studholme St, knits up wool spun down the line at Milton, Otago, in their signature possum and merino blend. Open seven days, (03) 689 7973. Those other Aussie imports, wallabies, have made a home in the hills behind this pretty town. There's a nice historical museum, too, in the grand old 1879 courthouse and surrounding historic structures at 28 Shearman St. www.waimatedc.govt.nz

Going South: Dunedin to Invercargill

At Three Mile Hill Rd, just seven minutes south of the city, Andy and Vicki of *Flagstaff Alpacas* have been breeding the fluffy creatures since 2001 — they now share their property with 175 of them. You can visit by appointment or even stay on the farm and enjoy the animals first-hand. Alpaca yarn is really luxurious to knit and wear — I can't wait to try some. (03) 476 7415, www.flagstaffalpacas.co.nz

The main street of Milton has a good antique shop called *Provincial Antiques*, some of whose treasures come from local estate auctions. They have very nice china, lots of linen and some vintage clothing, including fifties dresses — though not as much as they had on my last trip. I found a nice fifties rayon scarf to add to my collection, and was sorely tempted by a laundry basket full of hard-to-find vintage cotton sheets. Well worth stopping for — though not well signposted coming from the south. Look out for the sandwich board on the footpath. 84 Union St (the main highway), (03) 417 8841.

At the southern end of the main street is the quirkier *Walkers Trading*, on the corner of Ossian St — 'open most days, especially Friday, Saturday and Sunday'; (03) 417 8979.

Sadly Qualityarn's 1902 mill, where The Mill Factory Shop sold wool products to the public, closed in late 2011.

Further south, in the main street of Balclutha, is Angie's sweet wee *Bo Peep Wool Baa* at 27 Clyde St, (03) 418 2793.

Once known mostly as the home of country music in New Zealand, Gore is a thriving town that keeps adding interesting places to visit — the latest is the *Eastern Southland Art Gallery*, housed in an attractive 1909 converted Carnegie library building that Saatchi & Saatchi boss Kevin Roberts calls the 'Goreggenheim'. Just off the main street in the Arts and Heritage Precinct, the gallery houses a collection of Ralph Hotere's work gifted by the artist, works by Rita Angus and Theo Schoon, and an astonishing collection of mostly African art given by Janet Frame's mentor, John Money. Cnr Hokonui Dr and Norfolk St, just off the roundabout where the Invercargill-Dunedin road veers right. (03) 208 9907, www.goredc.govt.nz/artgallery

There's still good coffee at the *Green Room Café*, on the sunny side of the wonderfully named Irk St, which runs off at an angle from the main street. Nearby is *Gore May* deli.

Right across the street is Anne Baxter's *Jumper Co.* wool shop. A machine knitter from way back, Anne is doing more handknitting these days — and she really knows her yarns, including sock yarns. 14 Irk St, 021 180 4261.

A few doors along at 22 Irk St is Peter McGregor's toy and games shop *Only Kidding*. (03) 208 1290, www.onlykidding.co.nz

Gore girl Bronwyn Rabbidge went out on a limb when she bought an old villa to move her quilt business into. From an existing craft business in town with just 300 fabrics, *Nelly Applebys Quilt Store* now stocks 10 times that number and comfortably fills every room of the renovated house at 71 Hokonui Drive, on the corner of no-exit Howard St. (03) 208 6306, www.nellyapplebys.co.nz

New Zealand creative fibre tutor Biddy Kerr gave up a long time knitwear business in Gore to set up a studio 3 km out of town at 111 Racecourse Rd in a purpose-built barn. *Baa'n'Studio* is where she spins, dyes, knits, crochets, felts and teaches others about wool, including the fibre she shears from her coloured sheep. Biddy's an agent for Ashford spinning wheels and for Genesis, a dye-like colouring for fabric and fibre that needs no fixing. If you want to learn but don't live locally, she offers accommodation in her own home as well. (03) 208 6562, 027 233 4545.

Central Craftiness

En route to Queenstown and Wanaka from Dunedin, the pretty little Central Otago town of Lawrence — which at one stage had a population twice the size of Dunedin — has a great vibe and several good cafés. The bonus for crafty girls is the old Athenaeum Library, which has been refurbished as a weaving emporium. Professional weaver Lindy Chinnery has set up *The Textile Emporium and Weaving Studio* in the classic building — loom on one side, gloriously hued yarns, weaving, knitting, felting and embroidery, mostly from regional artisans, on the other. There are the lightest gossamer shawls to chunkier tweed lengths suitable for clothing. The Emporium is easy to find on the main street as you drive through to Wanaka at 9 Ross Place, (03) 485 9095, or email daisy5@vodafone.co.nz

Also in Lawrence is textile artist Angela Meecham, who works mostly in felt and dyed wool. Now with a studio at home, she is available for teaching and commissions, at 24 Harrington St, (03) 485 9364, or email art2enjoy@art2enjoy.co.nz

Chairmaker James Stewart, who crafts in the spirit of William Morris, is at home by appointment at 14 Campbellton St, Lawrence, (03) 485 9935 or 021 164 4512, chairmaker.tripod.com

Lawrence is positively humming with new life. They've put the power lines underground and the main street looks great. Liz Forbes' *O'Lea Home Collection*, housed in a lovely old brick building at 3 Ross Pl, has lots of pretty things for visitors to take home with them. (03) 485 9640, www.olea.co.nz. There are plenty of café options here too.

And, of course, there's Gabriels Gully nearby, where the first big goldrush took place.

Ask any crafty Otago woman for one out-of-town recommendation and she'll come up with *Touch Yarns*. This Alexandra company has relocated from an historic goldfields setting on Earnscleugh Rd into a showcase in Clyde, where Marnie Kelly's fine merino, Polwarth and kid mohair yarns will have you itching to stitch up a garment as soon as you fondle them. A spinner and weaver from way back, Marnie decided to concentrate on breeding sheep and goats that would produce fine fleece without the prickle factor that puts many people off wool. She now dyes her wool in an industrial area in Alexandra using, among other equipment, a dye plant from Kerikeri's Akatere Woolcraft (sorry Northland travellers!). The colours are gorgeous — the latest are inspired by Central Otago wildfowers, out in bloom on our trip — and the patterns distinctive; while Touch Yarns are exported internationally, the hand-dyed yarns make a fantastic gift for knitters overseas. Kits are available and there are needles, buttons, beads and threads too at the shop, which has expanded to include gifts and even a Christmas shop. Touch Yarns and Splurge, 27 Fache St, Clyde, (03) 449 2022, www.touchyarns.com. (Don't trust your GPS, you'll see it anyway opposite the back entrance to Olivers' Lodge & Stables, where I was hosted on my Central trip, (see page 240).

The drive through to Clyde was a revelation. Turning off at Milton, the road is at first narrow and winding with lots of little streams and masses of willows in fresh leaf. Then it starts to open up, passing through orchards, some still in flower — and covering more land than I'd dreamed of. I stopped to stretch my legs in Roxburgh, where the road veers west around the snow-covered Old

Man Range, and spotted an op shop still open. A wee hanky went into my bag to be washed and ironed later, as a souvenir of the day out.

The terrain becomes increasingly rugged as schist erupts through the dry hillsides in a beauty all its own. Road works offer the chance to look out on a tarn, so high it's almost at eye level. I loved this place! Barely have I passed through Alexandra when I reach Clyde, down off the new highway and above the river.

Frothy pink and white cherry blossoms line the avenue into the town, which almost died when the controversial dam was built just north of it. Now it's coming alive again as vineyards and cycle trails offer tourists new ways to appreciate the landscape and its bounty. Aucklanders David and Andrea Ritchie have joined in the regeneration of Clyde by renovating the Historic Places Trust Category One-listed buildings first made famous as *Olivers* by restaurateur Fleur Sullivan. They've started with the home built by Benjamin Naylor, who established a general store on the site in 1869 during the Otago goldrush, creating *Olivers' Lodge & Stables*. Their sensitive restoration of both house and stables offers restrained elegance with all the mod cons — in the lodge, bedrooms named for each of the families that have owned the property are decorated in restrained elegance, while the stables retain their rugged schist walls with a more playful style. I grabbed one of the bikes just returned from an Otago Rail Trail group and spent a pleasant half-hour before dinner familiarising myself with the layout of the town. (03) 449 2600, www.oliverscentralotago.co.nz

Next morning, fortified by a classic B&B breakfast, I headed through the Cromwell Gorge past the artificially raised Lake Dunstan. The vegetation has grown to soften the harsh edges; beehives are everywhere making the most of the flowering wild thyme. At Cromwell I called into the *Cider House Café & Bar* just over the bridge — recommended by fellow guests at Olivers — for coffee, and the Provisions shop — yes! they have wild thyme honey. The mountain ranges kept changing, though all were topped with snow from recent cold weather. Next stop was at *Gibbston Valley Cheese*, where I sampled feta and blue and bought a young goat's cheese for later. Another time this would be a great place to stop for a picnic with one of their platters. (03) 441 1388, www.gvcheese.co.nz

Then we're on to Arrowtown, en route to my flight home. There's plenty to explore in this charming historic goldmining village, from Chinese miners' cottages to an interesting array of shops. Allow time to have a good look around: this is a place well laid out for a stroll, especially in autumn when the poplars, too, turn to gold. Park down below the shops and walk around — there are galleries galore and plenty of foodie places. If you don't want to eat at a café, pick up some bread or sandwiches from the famous organic *Arrowtown Bakers* on the edge of town in Buckingham St, and take a picnic down to the water's edge. At the other end of the scale and just two doors along, in a corrugated-iron building tucked between old shops, is *Saffron* — winner of *Condé Nast Traveller*'s award for best restaurant in the district. It pays to book. (03) 442 0131, www.saffronrestaurant.co.nz

At the other end of the wee main street is the *Lakes District Museum,* open 9am to 5pm daily, (03) 442 1824. You might even strike a textile exhibition, as I did this time around with an Association of New Zealand Embroiderers' Guilds' national show. Down at street level below, you can even have your photograph taken in Victorian costume by Karen Reid; (027) 445 2569.

If you have time you can go to the movies in style in the comfortable, armchaired and licensed *Dorothy Brown's Cinema,* which has two theatres — the main one beautifully designed with Chinese silk ceilings, chandeliers and seriously spacious seats, and a smaller, more intimate space. There's also a bar that doubles as a bookstore. Open 10am till late every day in summer and from 11am in winter. (03) 442 1964, www.dorothybrowns.com

I found freshly baked goodies for my lunchtime flight back to Wellington at *Cook's Store & Deli,* which also sells tea towels and some vintage tablecloths. And of course there's the famous *Remarkable Sweet Shop,* full of holidaying school kids when we passed by.

Shops here are full of classy stuff. *Dreamz* has lovely luxury linens, while *Te Huia* has '100% New Zealand made' clothing, jewellery, leather, knitwear and home furnishings, and upstairs the gallery has good New Zealand art. (03) 442 1355 (choose option 2), www.thewoolpress.com/shop/ te-huia/. Furniture maker *Ed Cruikshank* showcases his stunning signature designs here at 50 Buckingham St, www.cruikshank.co.nz.

In one of several arcades behind shops, Pam Lawrence at *Blue Moon Rummage* is looking to build up her stock of found treasures, so watch this space. (03) 409 8000, www.bluemoonrummage.billboardme.co.nz

Sadly, said the local embroiderers I met looking after the exhibition at the museum, Destination Art on Ramshaw Lane, which looks out onto riverbank trees below the village, has gone. They go to Fabric Collections in Queenstown or the website set up by *Jan's Patch* after the shop closed, www.elna-janspatch.co.nz.

The Southern Lakes region has a stimulating sprinkling of crafty options. At *Christofer Robyn Quilts*, 641 Ballantyne Rd (airport end, 7 km from Wanaka), Chris Bartlett and Robyn van Reenen have a range of exciting patchwork fabric, exotic threads and books in their farm setting. They sell beads for embroidery and art quilt supplies. Their upstairs classroom-gallery also has an impressive view. Chris and Robyn will travel to teach or take classes locally. Robyn's husband Gilbert photo-graphs not only quilts but stunning landscapes too. Closed Sundays. (03) 443 1810.

Janice Jones sells her landscape-inspired quilts, vests, shawls, scarves and knitwear at *Fine Wools Wanaka*, 8 Helwick Street, (03) 443 7294, or you can visit her by appointment at 40 Kennedy Cr, (03) 443 7567.

In Wanaka township, at 62 MacPherson St, is another well-known textile artist inspired by the local landscape, quilter *Jeanette Gillies*. She will work to commission and can be visited by appointment. (03) 443 7774, gillies@wanaka.net.nz

Relishes Café on the lakefront road is open from 6pm for dining, in front of a cosy fire in winter or outdoors looking out at the lake in summer; 99 Ardmore St, (03) 443 9018. The *Artisans Studio* at 56 Ardmore St has work from 20 local artists and craftspeople. (03) 443 7578.

My favourite place to have coffee, indulge a sweet tooth and catch up on writing postcards is *Kai Whakapai*, on the waterfront at the corner of Ardmore and Helwick Sts. Upstairs there are stylish couches, plenty of cushions and a fireplace — with a fabulous view over the lake. Best value in town, I reckon. (03) 443 7795.

I sought a retreat on the banks of the Clutha in a classy restored villa offering a sunny verandah, a stunning outlook to the fast-flowing river and no more noise than the twitter of birds in a tree outside the bedroom window. Ann and Ian Horrax have created a retreat for even the most fussy bed-and-breakfast travellers without a huge price tag. It's stylishly furnished, books abound and the garden's a blossomed treat. Well-signposted, *Riversong* is only five minutes from Wanaka by car, at 5 Wicklow Tce, Albert Town, (03) 443 8567, www.riversongwanakaaccommodation.co.nz

Bernie Kiyabu and *Anne McNeill* have a gallery that's open by appointment out on Mt Barker Rd, just off the road to Queenstown via Cardrona. He is a woodturner and she is an artist who makes beautiful paper, as well as felting wool and silk garments, and art pieces. Ring first for directions. 590 Mt Barker Rd, RD2, Wanaka, (03) 443 7652. bgkiyabu@gmail.com

Queenstown Gems

Queenstown is stunningly situated — an amazing lake outlook, mountains at the far shores, the Remarkables, often covered in snow, behind you. Flying in or out can be a breathtaking experience, not only when range after range of mountains are snow-capped.

It's a pretty town too, with enough old buildings to foil the new ones, narrow streets running at odd angles and lots of cafés and boutiques as well as bike shops, ski shops and general outdoors stuff.

The town still has its all-day *Saturday market*, run by Creative Queenstown, down on the waterfront, selling work from spinners, knitters and felters, among other crafty artists. Follow the music for all the fun of the fair. May to October, 9am to 3pm, with longer hours in summer. Contact details on www.marketplace.net.nz

I found *Vesta*, a store specialising in New Zealand design and gifts, almost by chance, down on the waterfront. It's located in what is believed to be the oldest building in town, the 1864 Williams Cottage, a Category 1 Historic Place on the corner of (one-way) Earl St and 19 Marine Pde. A clever glass sliding door allows you to see out to the lake and mountains from the back of the house, where Andrew Murray has a small café with excellent coffee and food — which he serves in a conservatory in the front garden. I was fascinated by the variety of original wallpapers still adorning the scrim walls. (03) 442 5687, www.vestadesign.co.nz

Decode is a store with lots of goodies from New Zealand designers, which started out as fashion-only but has expanded to include jewellery, cushions — including Sue McMillan's Seam — and bedlinen by Paula Coulthard. It's at 13 Camp St, in the Post Office Precinct, just before the police station and the one-way loop leading down to Vesta. (03) 441 3094.

Bryn and Margaret Melhop have been in their *Fabric Collections*, at Shop 7, Gorge Rd Retail Centre — on the way to Arrowtown — for some years now, and their experience shows in the advice they give as well as their comprehensive stock. There's a great mix of fabrics — patchwork, some furnishing (including Kaffe Fassett) and dressmaking — as well as beads, braids, New Zealand-inspired fabric and kits, both trad cross-stitch and contemporary, and all the notions you need to stitch them up. I couldn't resist buying some lovely Japanese fabric to make granddaughter Olive Rose a pretty summer dress. 0800 732 274.

Textile artist *Sue Wademan*, an Australian by birth, and her English husband Spike have made Queenstown their home for 16 years now; you can visit her by appointment at The Studios, cnr Ballarat and Stanley Sts. (03) 441 3374, www.suewademan.com

Out at Tarras — where the road from Wanaka and the West Coast meets the Christchurch road — Christina Perriam now runs her mum Heather's *Merino Shop*, and a fashion store, part of a little cluster including a café and country store. The range of woollies is impressive and we were ready for a cuppa by the time we'd had a good look round. Open 9am to 5pm daily, (03) 445 2872, www.christinaperriam.co.nz. There's a Shrek museum too, and further up the road is the now-famous *Mrs Robinson*'s collectables shop. (03) 445 2210.

Into Invercargill

 Invercargill has some of the most extraordinary buildings I've seen on my travels — the 1915 First (Presbyterian) Church is the most ornate I've come across anywhere. There are more brick edifices than this Wellingtonian has ever seen, including the 1889 Water Tower on Queens Drive. *Queens Park* in the centre of the city is a great green reserve, and my wee eponymous motel on Alice St — a quiet, refurbished no-nonsense sort of place that's won awards — backed onto it, promising glorious walks ... if only it hadn't been raining cats and dogs. I saw one Labrador out with his master but I was not going to join them. (03) 214 4504, www.queensparkmotels.co.nz

Southland Museum and Art Gallery further around in the beautiful Queens Park is well worth a visit, and its setting is an added treat. Open daily except Christmas Day, (03) 219 9069, www.southlandmuseum.com

The city still retains the magic imbued by the filming of *The World's Fastest Indian* — in fact blokes might like to see the actual original motorbike at *E. Hayes & Sons*, 168 Dee St — claimed to be 'the ultimate blokes tool shop'. But Invercargill's recasting as a seat of learning has added a new dimension to the centre of town, with streets round the Southland Polytechnic buildings buzzing with young energy.

Invercargill is a hive of crafting activity, with a choice of wool and fabric shops to equip yourself for those cold southern nights. Many had moved since my last visit and some have closed, but others have grown.

That crafty Invercargill institution Whichcraft has, sadly, closed. However, Angela Carter's *Kitznthings*, formerly out in the country at Woodend, has grown enormously — the shop goes on forever. There was so much new stock just in from younger designers' ranges that they were out of boards and shelf space when I called! I must say the neatly folded stacks of fresh, often floral fabrics were very tempting — I wanted not only to pick them up and stroke them but to take them home! 152 Spey St, (03) 214 9111, www.kitznthingz.co.nz

Across the road at 147 Spey St is the *Seriously Good Chocolate Company*. They sell prettily patterned chocolates and will make you a hot beverage using their own product. (03) 218 8060, www.seriouslygoodchocolate.com

Glenda Carter's *Bernina Sewing Centre* has moved to 93 Yarrow St, cnr Deveron St, (03) 218 3398, near a *Save Mart* store and *hospice shop*. In fact, Invercargill's great place to op shop — when the town was overrun by film crews, the Sallies produced a typed list of 21 op shops for visitors to trawl through. I had a fantastic day finding blankets and other quiltable stuff last time around, but not this time.

Vintage store *Hubbers Emporium* still has a huge assortment of browseable goods at 68 Dee St, the main street that runs at right angles to most others in the CBD; (03) 218 8737.

Jan Gibb is a seasoned spinner, felter, knitter, dyer and all-round crafter who lives for her fibres, knows what she's selling and will teach workshops too. She and her husband Bill's home business *BJ's Colourways & Collectables* is located in the suburb of Grasmere at 21 Price St — the collectables are his Jaguar bits and pieces, and he'll happily make a cuppa for blokes while their women are out in the garage with Jan stroking the soft stuff. They welcome visitors between 9am and 5pm to check out Jan's enormous range of dyed and undyed wools, mohair, silk, nylon, rayon and cotton yarns for spinners and felters, and multi-coloured hand-dyed threads, dyes and a limited selection of cotton fabric for patchworkers. (03) 215 7667, jangibb@slingshot.co.nz

Not far from BJ's is textile artist Julie Hennessy, who's been an embroiderer 'forever'. She makes stitched, beaded jewellery, machine embroiders, does dressmaking and teaches classes, all from home at 345 Bainfield Rd, just on the edge of the rural delivery zone. Frustrated by the availability of the tiny seed beads she requires, Julie now imports them under her Seed and Bead Supplies brand. She also offers classes with accom-modation at the family's crib in Queenstown, and teaches at the annual Wanaka Embroidery School, run by the Otago Embroiderers' Guild. RD2, (03) 215 8074, juliefh@vodafone.co.nz

Jan and Bill are immediately behind *Café Greenworld,* in the old Lynwood Homestead right next to a plant nursery, which I visited last time I was in town. It's a good-value place popular with locals rather than tourists, fully licensed and open seven days, 8am to 4pm. 200 North Road (the extension of Dee St), (03) 215 8101.

Jan's friend Dawn Molloy is a felter from way back who sells her felted scarves, hats, mitts and jackets mostly at craft markets, but will welcome visitors by arrangement. *Felt-4-U Knits and Accessories,* (03) 217 7788.

Also nearby is dyer Shirley Goodwin, whose *Tillia Dyes & Fabrics* business was formerly based in Oamaru. She's at home at 10 Hensley St, Gladstone, (03) 214 7964, but ring first, as this is a mail-order business rather than a shop. www.tillia.co.nz

Out at the shops in suburban Windsor is *Found my Way*, a design store with lots of crafty goodness made in New Zealand, from baby gear to neat paper stuff. 38 Windsor St, (03) 217 7706.

It was hard finding anywhere to eat in Invercargill on a Monday night that wasn't a pub — until I remembered spotting an intriguing sign on the main road coming in from Queenstown. At first I wondered if I'd struck a club of some sort — it was all so low key, with 'rooms' curtaining off some large groups. But the waitress at *Buster Crabb* found me a quiet table and I enjoyed a chowder of local seafood. Why the genial host Alan Arnold should have chosen a British spy as his inspiration I still don't know — but this place had a pleasing ambience reminiscent of some of the capital's newer eating places, and I enjoyed the slight air of mystery that reading the back story didn't put to rest. 326 Dee St, Avenal, (03) 214 4214.

Next day, at Bluff, I found dollmaker Helen Back who has, typically, gone from one extreme to the other — she's moved from Karamea, at the top of the island, to Bluff, where she has opened a gallery called *Jimmi Rabbitz*. Don't be misled by the doll label — anyone who legally changes her name to one suggesting a tormented past has a wicked sense of humour. A sculptor for 14 years, Helen has also worked on short-film animation, and her finely detailed, quirky creations — much like something out of Hogarth's *Rake's Progress* — are regularly exhibited at galleries including *The Artist's Room* in Dunedin. She has a 'bread-and-butter' line of brightly coloured dancing dolls, makes saucy little nuns in boxes and will have a go at just about any commission. Ring first — if she's home she'll open up if she's not already open. 027 460 2873, www.helenback.com

Christmas Tree Mini Hangings

MATERIALS

Assorted 4.5 cm (1¾ inch) strips of coordinating fabrics for tree and trunk

Two 10 cm x 18 cm (4 x 7 inch) rectangles of fabric for background

One 6.5 cm (2½ inch) strip for binding

One 20 cm (8 inch) piece of iron-on pelon or scrap of batting

One 20 cm (8 inch) piece of fabric for backing

Decorative threads for quilting

DIRECTIONS

1. Piece together strips of fabric in four rows for the tree. Using a ruler and rotary cutter cut out a triangle shape using a 60-degree angle. The base of the triangle should measure 15 cm.
2. Attach the 10 cm x 18 cm triangles of background fabric to the sides of the tree. Trim the tree to 13 cm high and 16.5 cm wide.
3. Cut a 4.5 cm square of fabric for the trunk and two 4.5 cm x 7 cm pieces of background fabric to go either side of this.
4. Cut a 2.5 cm x 16.5 cm strip of background fabric and attach this to the base of the tree block.
5. Layer your tree, pelon and backing fabrics, and quilt through all three layers as desired.
6. Bind.

These can be strung together like bunting if desired.

DESIGNED BY: RACHEL ANN MAW OF ANNIE'S COUNTRY QUILT STORE

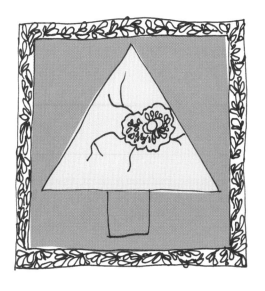

Events and Useful Information

National Organisations/Contacts/Events

Combined Textiles Guild — includes dyers, Box 268, Huntly.

Costume and Textile Association of New Zealand — includes curators, conservators, collectors, crafters and academics. Biennial symposium. www.costumeandtextile.co.nz

Creative Fibre — annual Festival, April/May, usually includes an exhibition and fashion award, www.creativefibre.org.nz

Dunkley's Great New Zealand Craft Shows — in 16 centres annually, with three in the Auckland region. Craft workshops, cooking demos and a huge line-up of crafty people, www.craftshows.co.nz

National Association of Dollmakers — www.dollfederation.co.nz

National Association of New Zealand Quilters Inc — Association of individual quilters, www.aotearoaquilters.co.nz

National Quilt Symposium — biennial, odd years. Month varies, according to host region's choosing. To be held in Taupo in 2013, www.tauposymposium.co.nz

New Zealand Association of Embroiderers' Guilds — biennial conference July, even years, www.anzeg.org.nz

New Zealand Association of Miniature Enthusiasts — biennial convention, even years, Labour weekend, www.nzame.org

New Zealand Lace Society — AGM April, alternates between North and South Islands, www.lacc.org.nz

SENZ — annual New Zealand stamping and
   scrapbooking event, www.senz.co.nz

Regional Events

Auckland

Auckland Art & Craft Fair — held biannually with one
   fair in winter and one in summer. A selection of
   New Zealand's best independent and contemporary
   designers, artists and crafters selling their products
   direct to the public for one day only,
   www.aucklandfair.blogspot.com
Auckland Dollmakers and Collectors Annual Doll Show —
   usually held in September, www.aucklanddollclub.co.nz
Auckland Vintage Textile Fair — annual, late August,
   Alexandra Park Raceway. Contact: Brian, 021 433 588;
   (09) 820 1900.
Calico Christmas — November, annual quilt show of the
   Auckland Patchworkers & Quilters Guild,
   www.apqg.co.nz
Crafternoon Tea Craft Market — held on the 3rd Saturday
   of every month from 10am-2pm,
   www.crafternoon-tea.blogspot.com
Kraftbomb — last Sunday of every month at Grey
   Lynn Community Centre in Auckland. An indie,
   alternative handcraft market supporting all things
   handmade and encouraging the use of traditional
   handcrafts and upcycling,
   www.kraftbomb.blogspot.com
The Devonport Craft Market — held on the first Sunday of
   every month from 10-3 in the summer and 10-2 in
   the winter, www.devonportcraftmarket.blogspot.com

Hamilton

Calling All Quilts — biennial, even years. Waikato
   Patchworkers and Quilters Guild gathering, quilt
   exhibition and craft merchants,
   www.whatsonhamilton.co.nz/eventlisting.aspx?id=3067

Doll and Teddybear Show — Hamilton Gardens Pavilion,
www.whatsonhamilton.co.nz/eventlisting.aspx?id=1865
New Zealand Craft and Quilt Fair — September,
Claudelands Events Centre, www.craftfair.co.nz

Cambridge
New Zealand Machine Quilters' Conference — biennial,
date changes, www.quiltique.co.nz

Tauranga
The Little Big Markets — Tauranga's monthly vintage
and crafty gatherings, cnr Maitai & Maunganui Rds,
thelittlebigmarkets.blogspot.com (hum-along to their
website!)

Opotiki
Opotiki Fibre and Fleece Fashion Awards and Exhibition —
July, showcases stunning items made from natural
materials, www.fibreandfleece.co.nz

Hawke's Bay
Fruit Bowl Craft Jam — a makers' market held each
December at Hawke's Bay Opera House, Hastings.

Palmerston North
Alt Shift Craft Markets — various dates throughout the
year, run by three Manawatu women for out-there
crafters to show and sell their unique, and original
crafts and arts, www.facebook.com/alt.shift.craft
Fabricabrac — annual, around August; fabulous fabric
buy, sell and swap with proceeds to Arohanui
Hospice, fabricabrac.wordpress.com
Tote & Gloat — May, Rose City Quilters,
www.rosecityquilters.blogspot.com
Yesterday's Treasures — annual sale of antique linen
and vintage and antique goods. St Paul's Church,
Broadway Avenue, March,
www.methodistsocialservices.org.nz/events/

Wairarapa

Craft Country Fair — from the collective that runs Featherston's Craft Country Shop, an annual fair offering contemporary, quality handmade products for all ages. Greytown Town Hall and Library, December, craftcountry.wordpress.com

New Rags Market Day — a monthly farmers' market for crafters and creatives' in the Masterton Town Hall, newragsmarket@gmail.com or Facebook.

Wellington

Craft 2.0 — quarterly, a craft fair for style junkies, craft enthusiasts and all fans of handmade. City Market, Undercover in the Atrium, Chaffers Dock Building, 1 Herd St, www.craft2.org/blog/

Eat, Drink & Be Crafty — once a year, Battle Hill Pauatahanui. Specialty craft event, www.eatdrinkcrafty.co.nz

Fabricabrac — twice yearly, a fabulous fabric buy, sell and swap with proceeds to Mary Potter Hospice at St Anne's School Hall, Newtown (also in Palmerston North and Sydney), www.fabricabrac.wordpress.com

Fabric Lovers' Market — Avalon (Taita) Intermediate, High St Lower Hutt, October, depending on school terms, (04) 567 7453.

Get Crafty on Logan — first Sunday of every month, Upper Hutt, www.facebook.com/getcraftyonlogan

Handmade — Queens Birthday weekend, 1st in June, a contemporary, creative and inspiring Wellington-wide weekend event full of activities covering many types of craft, www.handmade2012.co.nz

Just Good Stuff — a weeklong, pre-Christmas sale of crafty goodness at Thistle Hall Gallery, Upper Cuba St, justgoodstuffs.blogspot.com

Knack Craft Market — various dates throughout the year, range of New Zealand-made craft from vintage knits to hair accessories and jewellery. On facebook and at knackcraft.blogspot.com

Pataka, Porirua — the museum's annual Craft Market takes place each October. pataka.org.nz

World of Wearable Art —September, www.worldofwearableart.com

Christchurch

A Craft Affair (formerly Craft 2.0 Christchurch) — an indie craft market featuring a wide variety of handmade goods. Due to earthquake disruption, it was cancelled in 2011, www.acraftaffair.co.nz www.facebook.com/acraftaffair

Canterbury Modern Quilt Guild — part of an international movement. Meets 2nd Thursday monthly at Stitch Playroom, 27A Colombo St, Cashmere, (03) 332 1820, www.canterburymodernquiltguild.com

Crafty Business — first Monday of every month, a get-together to meet other crafters and discuss projects and problems, www.craftybusiness.co.nz

Creative Flair Fair — annual event bringing together merchants from around the South Island, exhibitions and workshops, www.creativeflairfair.blogspot.com

Culverden Country Fair — October, www.thefete.co.nz

The Craft Collective Markets — various dates throughout the year. The Craft Collective organises markets with locally made goods, vintage items, and food, www.facebook.com/thecraftcollectivenz

Stash reHash — occasional fabric market run by Arthritis New Zealand, stashrehash.wordpress.com

Sunday Artisan Market — Riccarton House & Bush, 16 Kahu Rd, (03) 348 6190.

Queenstown

Creative Queenstown Arts & Crafts Market — every Saturday on the lakefront, www.marketplace.net.nz

Wanaka

Wanaka Embroidery School — third weekend in March, run by the Otago Embroiderers' Guild since 1985. Contact: Eleanor Brown, (03) 467 2545, www.oegembroideryschool.co.nz

Wanaka Autumn School — April, includes textile arts,
www.autumnartschool.net.nz

Moxie Market — first Friday of every month, a market
with style offering a kaleidoscope of unusual, high-
quality, locally handmade creations,
moxiemarket.blogspot.com
www.facebook.com/moxiemarket

Retreats

Clements Hill Embroidery Retreat — homestay
accommodation an hour's drive from Auckland with
classes by award-winning embroider Val Waterhouse.
Prices by arrangement. (09) 422 5579,
info@clembroidery.co.nz
Stanford Retreats — former Cherry Pie Quilt Patch
owner Cheryl Chambers offers weekend retreats
with all food provided at 288 Arapaepae Rd, the
bypass road from Levin to Shannon. (06) 367 5220,
stanfordretreat@xtra.co.nz
Parklee Retreats — Karen Bird hosts quilt retreats as
well as assisting her husband with bullriding rodeos
at their Kimbolton farm near Feilding. She's also
happy to offer visiting quilters B&B as long as she's
not too busy. (06) 328 5881, bird@parklee.co.nz

Resources — Online and Mail Order

Beadaholic — New Zealand-based online retailer,
www.beadaholic.co.nz
Beading Divaz — mother-daughter team selling a large
selection online, www.beadingdivaz.com
Beads & Components for Jewellery — Annie Semmens &
Mandy Cunningham, (04) 977 2639,
bcfj@paradise.net.nz

Lucellan Living — Katya Gunn, 96 London St, Dunedin, (also see page 230), (03) 477 9944, www.lucellan.com
New Zealand Beading Supplies — www.newzealandbeadingsupplies.co.nz
The Bead Gallery — (also see page 174), www.beads.co.nz
Tiger Eye Jewellery & Beads — www.tigereyebeads.com
Zigzag Polymer Clay Supplies — for dollmaking, beads and other related products, www.zigzag.co.nz

Bears and bear-making

Bear Essentials — P.O. Box 363, Silverdale, Auckland, (09) 424 2015, www.bearessentials.co.nz
Hands Ashford NZ Ltd — online retailer of various craft products, including teddy-making supplies. Retail store 5 Normans Rd, Elmwood, Christchurch, (03) 355 9099, www.handscraftstore.com
Heatherbelle Bears — commission bearmaker, formerly the Bear Maker shop in Tirau, heatherbellebears@xtra.co.nz
Robin Rive Bears — (09) 527 8857, www.robinrive.com

Books

Minerva Textile Books and Gallery — craft, fashion, textile and quilter's bookshop, 237 Cuba St, Wellington, (04) 934 3424, www.minerva.co.nz

Children's crafts, clothing

babylicious.co.nz — the web business of Martha Craig and Glen Barris who own the Wanda Harland stores in Petone and Mt Victoria, Wellington.
Seedling — create kits that encourage creative thinking in kids, two stores in Auckland, products available online and throughout the country, www.seedling.co.nz
Silver Circus — Ange Holtslag sells her handmade children's clothing at Craft 2.0 and www.silvercircus.co.nz

Christmas ornaments and supplies

Christmas Treasures — online retailer of decorations, lights, ornaments and more, www.christmastreasures.co.nz

Santa's Choice — online Christmas supplies retailer, and Swiss chalet-style Christmas shop at 63 Egmont Rd, RD2, New Plymouth, (06) 755 1934, www.santaschoice.net.nz

The Christmas Heirloom Company — stores in Auckland, Hamilton, Palmerston North, Taihape, Tauranga, Tirau and Whangaparaoa, www.christmasheirloom.com

Craft, embroidery, patterns and kits, knitting supplies

2minuteneedles.com — two sisters wanted some big fat needles and could only import a bulk lot. They expanded their stock to include gems such as ebony sock needles.

acembroidery.com — Alice's Cre8ive Embroidery.

Countryside Needlepoint — New Zealand mail-order business for products related to embroidery, craft and art, www.ashtonglen.co.nz

Craft House — arts, crafts, scrapbooking, cardmaking and other craft products available online and at 47–53 Hutt Rd, Thorndon, Wellington (also see page 139), www.crafthouse.co.nz

Crafters Heaven — online retailer of craft supplies with a shop at 169 Main St, Greytown (also see page 155), (06) 304 8477, www.craftersheaven.co.nz

Craft-Search — online craft directory. nz.craft-search.com

Creative Craft Supplies — online retailer of craft supplies based at 20 Elliott St, Johnsonville, Wellington, (04) 477 1052, www.creativecraftsupplies.co.nz

Fionamarie.com — eclectic mix of patchwork, stitchery, doll and cloth creation patterns from New Zealand and Australian designers.

House on the Hill — American and French country-style fabrics, patterns and art. 25 Konini St, Christchurch (also see page 209), (03) 348 2361, www.houseonthehill.co.nz

Jane Van Keulen — textile artist and educator, and supplier of hand-dyed threads (also see page 219), www.janevk.com

JJ's Crafts Ltd — online and store at 14 Gloucester St, Greenmeadows, Napier (also see page 88), (06) 844 0680, www.jjscrafts.co.nz

Screenmaker — makes screens ready for printing from your image or text, www.silkscreenmaker.com

Strand Natural Fibres Ltd — New Zealand mohair/wool embroidery thread and needlework kits, www.strandnz.com

Susan Claire — online retailer Susan Claire Mayfield runs her business out of Toad Hall, her home in a big old villa on the outskirts of Otaki, north of Wellington. Quilting materials, accessories and patterns, www.susanclaire.com

The Embroiderer — needlework store based in Birkenhead with products also available online (also see page 37), www.theembroiderer.co.nz

The Fox Collection — online retailer of needlework and craft supplies, including stitching frames, www.thefoxcollection.co.nz

The Threaded Needle — embroidery and cross-stitch product suppliers, along with general craft supplies, www.thethreadedneedle.co.nz

Web Stitch — cross stitch, patchwork quilt, cushion and cloth doll patterns and kits, www.webstitch.co.nz

Dollmaking

Cloth Doll Connection — cloth doll designers and links to patterns and suppliers, www.clothdollconnection.com

Dollworld — Hamilton-based online retailer of doll-making supplies. Website also includes tutorials, www.dollworld.co.nz

The Doll Supplies Company — online retailer of dolls by Shirley Johnston and doll-making accessories, www.dollsuppliescompany.co.nz

Dyes, paints, dyed and painted fabrics

Ashford Handicrafts Ltd — based in Ashburton, make a range of spinning, weaving and carding equipment and supply dyes, yarn, fibre and books (also see page 213), www.ashford.co.nz

Creative Outlet — textiles, dyes, yarns and patterns. Website also includes tips and free patterns, www.creativeoutlet.co.nz

Hands Ashford NZ Ltd — 5 Normans Rd, Elmwood, Christchurch (also see page 205), (03) 355 9099, www.handscraftstore.com

JJ's Crafts Ltd — online and store at 14 Gloucester St, Greenmeadows, Napier, (also see page 88), (06) 844 0680, www.jjscrafts.co.nz

Plume Art Limited — Jenny Hunter's fine textile art supplies and books, www.plumeart.co.nz

Spectrum Hand Dyed Fabrics — fabrics designed by Mieke Apps (also see page 18), www.spectrumfabric.co.nz

Teri Dyes — David Harding & Katharine McHardie's Woodville-based business selling dyes for flax, animal fibres and cotton, www.teri-dyes.co.nz

Tillia Dyes & Fabrics — dyes, paints and fabrics as well as online tutorials (also see page 251), www.tillia.co.nz

Zigzag Polymer Clay Supplies — also supply fabric paints and dyes, and fibres, www.zigzag.co.nz

Fabric

Bolt of Cloth — bold and beautiful fabrics from designers in New Zealand, Australia and abroad available both online and in-store at The Colombo Mall, 363 Colombo St, Christchurch (also see page 210), www.boltofcloth.com

fabricfixation.co.nz — Tauranga-based online business specialising in high-quality, contemporary designer fabric and accessories.

Fabric Online — Christchurch-based online retailer of cotton fabrics, www.fabriconline.co.nz

Felt Supplies of NZ Ltd — suppliers of industrial-weight felt, (09) 813 4664, feltsuppliesnz@xtra.co.nz

Fionamarie.com — patchwork quilting supplies and
fabrics, patterns from New Zealand and Australian
designers.
Global Fabrics — top quality designer dress fabrics, stores
in Auckland, Wellington, Christchurch, Dunedin,
Sydney and Melbourne (also see pages 33 and 130),
www.globalfabrics.co.nz
Kiwi Threadz Ltd — Pukekohe-based quilting fabric and
supplies, www.kiwithreadz.com
Martha's Furnishing Fabrics — curtain and upholstery
fabrics from mills in Europe and America, store in
Auckland (also see page 42), www.marthas.co.nz
Sentosa Textiles — online supplier of fabrics, yarns,
textiles and fibres based in Auckland,
www.sentosatextiles.com
sewaddictivefabrics.co.nz
Sew Pretty — Christchurch-based Kirsty Hocking's
website, www.sewpretty.co.nz
Stitchbird Fabrics — Wellington-based, retro and vintage-
style fabrics and sewing accessories,
www.stitchbirdfabrics.co.nz
ThumpaCat Fabrics — online retailer with a huge selection
of fabrics, www.thumpacat-fabrics.co.nz

Knitting yarns and raw fibre

Alterknitives — designer yarns for the contemporary
knitter, Herne Bay, Auckland (also see page 35),
(09) 376 0337, knitit@ihug.co.nz
Anna Gratton Ltd — boutique mill and farm shop,
Dunolly Rd, Waituna West, RD 9, Feilding,
(06) 328 6868, www.annagratton.co.nz
Artisan Fibres — online fibre shop formerly in the
Christchurch Arts Centre, www.artisanfibres.co.nz
Brenel Alpacas — alpaca fibre and yarn, knitting kits and
patterns, www.brenelalpacas.co.nz
Briar Patch — 100 per cent pure New Zealand knitting
wool, www.briarpatch.co.nz
Chocolate Wool NZ —naturally coloured wool from Gotland
sheep; also farm visits. Pleasant Valley, Palmerston,
South Island, www.chocolatewoolnz.50webs.com

Felt and Fibre — dying, carding and felting services.
7 Methven Highway, Allenton, Ashburton,
www.feltandfibre.co.nz

Kane Carding — Greytown-based specialists in
commission carding and suppliers of quality wools
for spinning and felting, www.kanecarding.co.nz

Knit World — www.knitting.co.nz

Knitcola Stitchery (formerly Ashford Craftshop) — on the
main road in Ashburton. Large range of yarns, fibre
and books (also see page 213), (03) 308 9085,
www.ashford.co.nz

Knitsch — Tash Barneveld's dyed in Wellington New
Zealand wool sock yarn business, www.knitsch.co.nz

Misty Ridge Alpacas — alpaca breeders at Kaiwaka, 30 km
north of Napier, www.mistyridgealpacas.co.nz

Mohair Craft New Zealand — family-owned business
providing products made from mohair, possum and
merino. Stores in Pokeno, Dairy Flat and Papakura,
also on website, www.mohair.co.nz

New Zealand Alpacas Limited — supply greasy or
pre-carded fibre on request. 787 State Highway 1, RD2
Cambridge, www.nzalpacas.com

Riverdale Alpacas Mill & Shop — situated just outside
Otorohanga, supplies fibres, wool and garments,
www.riverdalealpaca.co.nz

Rotocard — fibre products, washing and carding services.
322 Old Coach Rd, Mahana, RD1, Nelson,
www.rotocard.co.nz

Skeinz — top-quality yarns from Napier-based business
that hit the headlines when it called for pyjamas
for penguins affected by the Rena oil spill (also see
page 88), www.skeinz.com

South Seas Knitting — Auckland-based online store
stocking a hand-picked selection of artisan yarns,
books, patterns and tools such as bamboo and rosewood
knitting needles, www.southseasknitting.com

Southern Alpacas Stud — situated on outskirts of
Christchurch, alpaca products available on website,
www.alpacasnz.co.nz

spinningayarn.co.nz — Jessica Win's fabulous batch-dyed
   fibres and yarn.
Stansborough Farms — yarn, accessories and garments
   (also see page 142), www.stansborough.co.nz
Stuart and Sue Albrey — RD9,Waimate, (03) 689 2704,
   www.fffnz.com
Tai Tapu Wool Carders — PO Box 56,Tai Tapu, Canterbury,
   (03) 329 6859
Tally-ho Natural Coloured Wools — online or at the shop,
   95 Scotland St, Roxburgh,
   www.tallyhowoolcarding.webs.com
Tauranga Knitting Centre — supplier of yarns and
   other knitting products both online and in-store at
   8/152 11th Avenue, 11th Avenue Plaza, Tauranga
   (also see page 62), www.taurangaknitting.co.nz
The Shearing Shed —angora fibre products, Waitomo
   Caves Rd, Waitomo, Waikato,
   www.angorashearingshed.co.nz
The Wool Shop — Torea St, Utiku, off SH1, 0800 607 010,
   www.thewoolcompany.com
The Yarn Queen — specialist New Zealand knitting
   business supplying yarns, books, patterns and tools
   online, www.theyarnqueen.co.nz
Thickthorne Llamas — llama and blended knitting yarns.
   The Cottage, Waikawa Valley, The Catlins,
   www.thevalleybeyond.com
Touch Yarns — Alexandra-based online retailer of fine
   New Zealand merino wool for knitting, weaving,
   embroidery and felting. Shop at Clyde (also see
   page 239), www.touchyarns.com

Quilting and quilting accessories

Annie's Country Quilt Store — sells everything related
   to quilting both online and from a store at
   167 Archibald St, Ashburton (also see page 212),
   www.anniesquilts.co.nz
Cushla's Village Fabrics — stores in Auckland and Waihi,
   selling fabric, patterns, books and more (also see
   page 39), www.cushlasvillagefabrics.co.nz
Grandmother's Garden — fabric, patterns, kitsets and

books for quilters (also see page 69),
www.grandmothersgarden.co.nz

Nolting Quilting System — www.quiltique.co.nz

powerquilter.co.nz — Russell-based Caroline Pyne

Quilters Dream New Zealand — online retailer of fabrics,
books, kits, patterns, threads and sewing machines.
Site also includes links to classes and groups,
www.quiltersdreamnz.com

quiltique.co.nz — long-arm quilters by region

Quilt Works — online retailer with a shop at 29 River
Terrace, Waipukurau, Hawke's Bay (also see page 94),
www.quiltworks.co.nz

Stitchworks — quilting website supplying a full range
of quilting products and services (also see page 64),
www.stitchworks.co.nz

Swiftquilter — 5 Eric Price Ave, Takapuna, Auckland,
(09) 486 6047, www.swiftquilter.co.nz

The Quilter's Shed — online retailer dedicated to
supplying patterns for quilts, dolls and more,
www.thequiltersshed.co.nz

Sewing machines, cabinets & accessories

Bernina — www.bernina.co.nz

Brother — www.brother.co.nz

Horn Sewing Cabinets — www.horn.com.au

Husqvarna — www.husqvarnaviking.com

Janome — www.janome.co.nz

Pfaff — www.pfaff.com

Sew Ezi — portable sewing tables, www.sewezi.co.nz

Terry Apparel Limited — industrial and domestic sewing
threads, needles and sewing accessories,
www.terryapparel.co.nz

Treadle On (The Southern Outpost) — 'People-powered'
treadle and hand-crank sewing machines and the
people who use them, www.treadleon.net.nz

Wellington Sewing Services — sell Janome, Elna, Pfaff,
Husqvarna, Singer, Baby Lock and repair all brands of
machine. Shop 3, Kilbirnie Plaza, 22 Bay Rd, Kilbirnie,
Wellington, www.sewingdirect.co.nz

Spinning wheel suppliers

Baynes Spinning Wheels — established in 1974, based in Ashburton. Manufacture popular wheels for spinners, www.spinning.co.nz

Knitcola Stitchery (formerly Ashford Craftshop) — on the main road in Ashburton. A range of spinning, weaving and carding equipment, dyes, yarn, fibre and books (also see page 213), (03) 308 9085, www.ashford.co.nz

Majacraft — Tauranga-based, family-owned and -operated company making double treadle spinning wheels. List of dealers on their website, www.majacraft.co.nz

Wheels and Whorls — online New Zealand stockists of fibre craft supplies including spinning wheels, drop spindles, weaving looms and more, www.wheelsandwhorls.co.nz

Stamping and scrapbooking

Create — scrapbooking, card making and paper craft studio and shop at 519 Mt Albert Rd, Three Kings, Auckland (also see page 45), www.create.net.nz

Creative Bugs — small online retailer of scrapbooking tools and products, www.creativebugs.co.nz

Just Scrapping — online retailer of wide range of quality scrapbooking products, www.justscrapping.co.nz

Hastings Rubber Stamps — wide selection of art stamps and paper craft goods available both online and in store at 416W Heretaunga St, Hastings (also see page 92), www.hasrub.co.nz

Rubbadubbadoo — quality handmade New Zealand art stamps available online. Workshop visits by appointment, 248 Grey St, Hamilton East, (05) 086 97826 (also see page 57), www.rubbadubbadoo.com

Rubber Stamps by Montarga — make own range of craft stamps and custom stamps to order. Catalogue and order forms online, shop at 165 Ferry Rd, Christchurch (also see page 209), www.artstamps.co.nz

Stamp Zone — Kay and Colin Dixon, Unit 9, 36 William
  Pickering Dr, North Harbour, (09) 414 4100,
  stampz@ihug.co.nz

Further reference

Websites

Aotearoa Quilters — formed in 1994 as the National
  Association of New Zealand Quilters (NANZQ),
  offers classes, exhibitions and professional
  development opportunities to quilters and textile
  artists, www.aotearoaquilters.co.nz
Clever Bastards — a New Zealand website promoting the
  work of clever Kiwi crafters, www.cleverbastards.co.nz
Etsy — online international craft marketplace and
  community of artists and crafters, including
  handknitter extraordinaire Lisa Jones:
  www.superlative.etsy.com, www.etsy.com
Felt — New Zealand-based online marketplace for
  handmade goods, designed to enable artists,
  designers and craftspeople to promote their work
  and connect with buyers. The forums are great for
  finding out what's happening, getting word out about
  an event, and discussing crafty issues, www.felt.co.nz
myantiqueshops.co.nz — without doubt the best online
  guide to New Zealand (and some overseas) antiques
  and collectable shops from an American now living
  in Wellington.
Ravelry — a place for knitters, crocheters, designers,
  spinners, weavers and dyers to keep track of their yarn,
  tools, project and pattern information, and look to
  others for ideas and inspiration. All content is user-
  driven and membership is free, www.ravelry.com
Textile Links — a comprehensive but not always reliable
  list of wool shops in New Zealand and Australia,
  textilelinks.com/com/shop/intlaus.html#countryNZ

Blogs

Birdspoke — sketches, stitches and models (mostly of birds) by Rachelle Wood, www.birdspoke.blogspot.com

Handmade Love —Australia-based artist, illustrator, art teacher and knitter Dawn Tan's work, www.hand-made-love.blogspot.com

Harvest Textiles — team of three women based in Melbourne who share a passion for quality handmade textiles, www.harvesttextiles.com.au

Glorybox — Kerryn Pollock's musings for vintage fabric and textile lovers are a virtual trousseau, gloryboxtextiles.wordpress.com

Kiwiyarns Knits — an ex-pat returns home to knit another day, kiwiyarns.wordpress.com

Mary Englebreit — for some years a must-have mag for crafters, *Mary Englebreit's Home Companion*, has sadly died. But you can still catch up with her blog and buy her products — including a notebook proclaiming Arts and Crafts Keep You Sane at maryenglebreit.com

NZ Felters — a group of felt makers from all over the country who share a passion for creating with wool and fibre. Affiliated with Creative Fibre, www.nzfelters.blogspot.com

New Zealand Handmade — supports independent craftspeople, artisans and designers prodasucing New Zealand-made, quality goods. Also has a good listing of craft events around the country, www.newzealandhandmade.co.nz

Stamp Happy — blog of Stampin' Up Independent Demonstrator, Jaquelyn Pederson. Good source of info about scrapbooking events, workshops and tips and techniques, www.stamphappy.co.nz

Magazines

Extra Curricular — published tri-annually, put together in Auckland for and about people doing exciting side projects in their spare time, www.extracurricularmag.blogspot.com

Frankie — bi-monthly magazine published in Australia that includes craft ideas and stories, as does their website, www.frankie.com.au

New Zealand Quilter — not just quilts and quilters' stories, www.nzquilter.com

The Gift of Stitching — a monthly e-zine set up by Australia-based Kirstan Edwards, www.thegiftofstitching.com

Books

Crafted by Design, Jeanette Cook and Stephen Robinson, Random House New Zealand, Auckland, 2005. Includes textile artists.

Stitch: Contemporary New Zealand Textile Artists, Ann Packer, Random House New Zealand, Auckland, 2006.

Stitch 'n' Bitch, Debbie Stoller, Workman Publishing, New York, 2003. A practical and funny book on knitting.

The Loving Stitch: A History of Knitting and Spinning in New Zealand, Heather Nicholson, 1998. Academic but essential history of Kiwi woolcraft.

Thrift to Fantasy, Rosemary McLeod, HarperCollins, Auckland, 2005.

Warm Heritage: Old Patchwork Quilts and Coverlets in New Zealand and the Women Who Made Them, Pamela Fitz Gerald, Bateman, Auckland, 2003. A history of patchwork quilting in New Zealand.

Thanks to

My hosts: Hathaway House, Stratford; Abel Tasman Marahau Lodge, Marahau; Straw Lodge, Marlborough; Belmont B&B, Christchurch; Cheltenham House, Hanmer Springs; Wisteria Cottage, Wakefield; Olivers Central Otago, Clyde; Robyn Croft; Helen & Stephen Packer; and my dad, Harley Taylor.

Jenny Hellen and Alexandra Bishop of Random House for giving *Crafty Girls* another day out. Special thanks also to Tom Blacker and Kimberley Davis at Random House for fact checking and appendices — what a marathon!

Pieta Brenton, Deborah Smith, Mark Smith and Lorraine Smith for the gorgeous vintage design, photography and illustrations.

Ace Rentals, again, for the cars.

The late and much missed Bub Bridger for her poem *At the Conference*.

Anna Prussing and Sarah De Renzy — sisters in stitch for over two decades.

Genevieve Packer, a crafty daughter who never ceases to surprise and inspire me.

Peter Freer for IT help and my husband Den for his support.

And to the many stitchers who live on in fond memories and through their textiles, especially Malcolm Harrison, Isabel McIlraith, and my mother Betty Taylor. *Miss you.*